THE
DOG DIET
ANSWER BOOK

THE
DOG DIET
ANSWER BOOK

=== THE COMPLETE NUTRITION GUIDE TO HELP YOUR DOG ===
LIVE A HAPPIER, HEALTHIER, AND LONGER LIFE

GREG MARTINEZ, DVM

FAIR WINDS

In memory of Elizabeth "Betsy" Gammons

Quarto is the authority on a wide range of topics.

Quarto educates, entertains and enriches the lives of our readers—enthusiasts and lovers of hands-on living.

www.QuartoKnows.com

© 2016 Quarto Publishing Group USA Inc.

First published in the USA in 2016 by
Fair Winds Press, an imprint of
Quarto Publishing Group USA Inc.
100 Cummings Center
Suite 406-L
Beverly, MA 01915-6101
QuartoKnows.com
Visit our blogs at QuartoKnows.com

20 19 18 17 16   1 2 3 4 5

ISBN: 978-1-59233-702-6   **33614059941814**

Digital edition published in 2016
eISBN: 978-1-62788-788-5

Library of Congress Cataloging-in-Publication Data available.

Cover and book design by Leigh Ring // www.ringartdesign.com
Photographer credits shutterstock.com

Printed and bound in China.

The information in this book is for educational purposes only. It is not intended to replace the advice of a veterinarian. Please consult your pet's health care provider before beginning any new health program.

CONTENTS

INTRODUCTION

DECIDING WHAT TO FEED YOUR DOG CAN BE CONFUSING AND INTIMIDATING, ESPECIALLY AS YOU BROWSE LONG STORE AISLES OF BAGS, CANS, AND COOLERS OF ALL TYPES OF DOG FOOD. This book will help you to decipher the long lists of ingredients and confusing labels. As you better understand dog food, you'll be able to keep your dog healthier and happier and address health issues by buying different types of food or adjusting the ingredients.

As a veterinarian, I did not always pay close attention to the type of food and treats that my patients ate. In veterinary school, I was taught that the number of food-associated medical problems in dogs was low, and so I assumed most allergies and medical issues were due to things other than sensitivity to food ingredients. When a dog was itchy, for example, I advised the client to use flea control and bathe the dog weekly with conditioner to remove pollens and other outside allergens. Only after I ruled out flea problems and environmental sensitivities would I consider a prescription diet to rule out anything else.

After reading *The Omnivore's Dilemma* by Michael Pollan, I began eating less processed food and more vegetables, fruits, and nuts. I lost weight, felt better, and had more energy. Pollan's perspective made me question the effect the processed, dry dog foods might be having on my patients. Maybe there was a food-based solution to the chronic skin, ear, and bowel ailments that are so commonly seen in veterinary practice. Could a grain-free, gluten-free diet paired with healthy treats, more oils, and a bit of healthy "human food" mixed in help these conditions? (Vets are known to scold their clients for feeding their dogs human food, while in reality, table scraps and sharing home-cooked food with our dogs was the norm for many years until commercial dog food became available.)

I started testing my theories with my own dogs. Carly, my Dalmatian, had been vomiting twice weekly for years. Archie, my tan, wirehaired terrier cross, suffered from petit mal seizures. Once I changed their diets to grain- and gluten free, these problems soon became a thing of the past. After witnessing the healing of my own dogs, I prescribed a gluten-free diet to all my patients' dogs and was amazed to see the medical benefits of a better diet. This inspired me to make ingredient checklists a standard part of my practice, and I encourage my clients to do the same for their pets. I am convinced that the ingredients we feed our pets has a greater impact on their health than what I was originally taught in veterinary school, and I cannot bear to see more pets suffer from eating the wrong ingredients in their food or treats. Did you know that the ingredients in the dog food are much more important than the brand?

Choosing the right diet for your dog may require some trial and error. There are so many choices, so many brands, and so many nutritional promises that the options can seem overwhelming—especially when you can't believe everything you read. Did you know that any commercial dog food can be labeled super premium without being of premium or, for that matter, even average quality? Put on your reading glasses, and I will help you decode the real information you need to make dog-diet decisions: the ingredients on the label, not the promises on the packaging.

DOCTOR'S NOTE

Watch for signs that your dog is not tolerating its food. Know every ingredient in the food, treats, and chews you give to your dog. The wrong ingredients can cause obesity, dry skin, severe itching, or diarrhea. The right ingredients can help a pet look and feel great.

After years of research, classes, and personal experience with veterinary nutrition, I have a deep understanding of dog food ingredients and health-specific diets for your furry family member. The wrong ingredients and cheaper diets may save you money in the beginning, but they can cost more in the end due to repeated visits to the veterinary hospital. While some dogs seem to thrive on just about any diet, others are very sensitive about what is put in their bowl. If you address the amount of calories, moisture, oils, and allergens in your dog's diet, you may see an animal go from chronically ill to the picture of health. Even if your dog seems OK with whatever you give it, food with fewer synthetic ingredients, fewer preservatives, and less processing is better for all dogs, period.

TREATING OBESITY

Foods in the marketplace have changed in recent years to address the needs of the growing number of overweight dogs. Dogs that carry around lots of extra weight can experience many health issues, such as arthritis and diabetes. In fact, a veterinary study showed that obese dogs may lose as much as eighteen months of life—and that doesn't even address the pain and potential medical treatments they have to endure for other conditions related to obesity. (You'll learn about calculating your dog's ideal weight in later chapters.) As a result of these obesity cases, there is a greater emphasis on preventing and treating obesity in our veterinary community.

ADDRESSING ALLERGIES

Skin allergies typically fall into three distinct categories: flea bites; allergies to pollens, molds, and grasses (atopic or contact allergies); and food allergies. Each type of allergic condition affects a different area, but all of them depend on how prone the skin is to inflammation. In my work, I've found that if the skin is healthy, then it may not react to allergens as much, and a diet with the right ingredients is key to that.

For many dogs, skin and ear misery may be partially due to a lack of healthy oils in their diet. A flea bite or cloud of pollen may not trigger a cascade of itching despair if the skin is protected by a natural layer of oil. In mild cases of any skin allergy, healthy oils and novel proteins (a protein your dog has never eaten before) in the diet may help relieve the issue as much as prescribed medications. And while food allergies are said to account for only a small percentage of all skin and ear problems that occur in dogs, there are now many grain-free foods and limited-ingredient diets for dogs that can't tolerate common types of allergenic ingredients such as wheat, beef, chicken, and dairy.

DEMYSTIFYING DOG DIETS

I'll talk throughout the book about the general categories of dog food, labeling, descriptions, and the ingredients in dog food. I'll explain the differences and similarities between dry, canned, dehydrated, raw, freeze-dried, refrigerated, and home-cooked diets; why we feed treats; and how to safely share healthy human food with our furry friends. Once you feel more comfortable with the choices available, you will be able to ask specific questions to find what you need. Instead of asking a sales associate, "What is the best dog food?" you will learn to say, "My dog has food allergies, occasional gut issues, and has had pancreatitis. Where is your limited-ingredient, lower-fat food?"

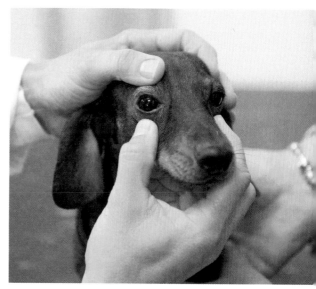

The proper diet for your dog should be based on his weight, tolerance or allergies to ingredients, and any medical issues he may have.

Making small changes in your dog's diet can make all the difference by restoring health, increasing energy, and giving your dog a better life without medical problems.

Sometimes, little ingredient tweaks can make a world of a difference in a dog's health. Simply changing the moisture content or ingredients in any type of food (canned, dry, raw, dehydrated, or home cooked) may help prevent needless suffering. Chronic skin, ear, or bowel problems may finally fade away. Excess weight, urinary crystals, terrible coat condition, and even seizures can sometimes dramatically respond to a few small changes.

Not every dog responds to dietary therapy, but the odds are pretty good that your dog will benefit in some way: 50 percent of dogs improve to some degree, while 10 to 20 percent dramatically improve, and 30 to 40 percent show either a decrease in symptoms or a reduction in the frequency of flare-ups from a medical issue. Improvement may mean that some dogs will need to stick to a more expensive or a prescribed diet, but they may ultimately need less medicine in their lifetimes.

I will also address a number of myths and confusing issues. For example, you may have heard that raw food and bones can be dangerous to feed our dogs. But this is not always true. Early on in my career, a well-known trainer and dog-show judge showed me that feeding dogs chicken necks can cut down on tartar buildup. Following her example, I have often fed my dogs frozen chicken wings for dental health or pieces of raw chicken, pork, shrimp, or cooked salmon fillets as a nutritious treat. In the chapters to follow, we will discuss not only the dangers of raw food and bones, but also when and where feeding raw bones or food to your dog may be appropriate and really healthful.

TODAY'S DOG

The commercialization of dog food has led to pampered pets that no longer have to hunt or scavenge. Their food is delivered to them once or twice daily. We also take our dogs on trips and to daycare and dog parks, and they receive grooming and excellent medical care. But the pampered-dog lifestyle has led to the overfeeding of our pets, creating an epidemic of obesity that is just as dangerous as the lack of calories that their ancestors often faced in the wild. In later chapters, I'll talk about how dog food is made, the evolution of better products, and major companies that own the industry.

When it comes to this readily available, mass-produced food, are all brands created equal? And are the ingredients in these brands good enough for our pets? Opponents to commercial dog food claim that diseased and cancerous meat, road kill, euthanized pets, disgusting parts of animals, fillers, and dangerous preservatives are used by manufacturers. I believe that while some or all those things may have been and are still used in cheaper products, the ingredients used in more expensive commercial dog food has gotten much better. In fact, some brands are made of human-grade ingredients. Learn more about high-quality ingredient pet foods at your local pet store or in the Resources section, page 183.

GETTING THE ANSWERS YOU NEED

Depending on the type and mix of ingredients, different kinds of commercial foods may lead to weight gain and medical problems such as obesity, skin issues, ear infections, and bowel issues.

If your dog was suffering from a medical issue and a diet could make a difference, can you envision feeding it a more expensive commercial food, dehydrated food, raw food, or home-cooked food? Or maybe even just sharing some of your dinner with your dog?

There are a few factors you need to consider when deciding what to feed your dog. Better quality commercial, raw, and dehydrated foods are more costly. Home cooking may cost as much as better quality foods, and it requires the additional time to buy and cook the ingredients. Home cooking also takes commitment to varying ingredients and adding supplements, as well as consulting with a veterinary nutritionist (or by using a website such as balanceIT.com) to make sure the diet is nutritionally complete.

A dog with medical issues or sensitivities may require a more expensive, limited-ingredient commercial diet; a veterinary prescription diet; or a specific home-cooked diet. Weight-challenged dogs or dogs prone to pancreatitis may need a lower-fat diet, and dogs with kidney problems may need a high-quality diet with slightly lower protein.

All these factors may seem overwhelming, but can be easily sorted out as you learn more about ingredients in different kinds

Diets should be determined not just by the size and breed of a dog, but by each dog's needs and reactions to food. Some do well with a bag of commercial kibble, while others require a prescription diet.

DOCTOR'S NOTE

My experiences with different foods have taught me to be open to the many ways to feed dogs. Feeding different brands and types of foods helps protect your pet from nutritional issues or processing problems (contaminants or toxins) with any one brand.

of dog food. We'll also learn how those different ingredients in the mix can cause or cure common medical conditions. I'll talk about how different diets may help.

EVERY DOG IS DIFFERENT

Some dogs seem to thrive on economy commercial foods, while others need expensive, limited-diet, canned food or a prescription food. This book isn't meant to be an alternative to your vet, a veterinary specialist, or a veterinary nutritionist. Instead, it is intended to help you understand how different ingredients may affect your dog's health. As our level of care for animals rises, and as available diagnostics expand, so has a vet's ability to treat complex medical problems. For those who can't afford the costly medical screening and testing, dietary changes may help solve, or partially solve,

a problem. However, don't ignore signs that tell you that dietary changes aren't working or that things are getting worse. A medical exam can provide reassurance that the changes are going in the right direction.

After reading this book, my hope is that you will feel much more informed about choosing the right ingredients to nourish your dog, and you will be more comfortable with feeding commercial, refrigerated, dehydrated, raw, canned, freeze-dried, prescription, or home-cooked food.

≡ CHAPTER 1 ≡
KEY INGREDIENTS
IN A DOG'S DIET

EVEN THOUGH DOGS MAY HAVE INDIVIDUAL NEEDS, THERE IS A GENERALLY ACCEPTED MIX OF FOOD INGREDIENTS THAT KEEP MOST DOGS HEALTHY AND HAPPY. Where did that recipe of meat, fat, grain, and other carbohydrates originally come from? Who in the world figured out the percentages of nutrients and the list of best ingredients to feed our loving companions?

To figure that out, we'll have to go back thousands of years to the time when the ancestors of our wonderful pets decided to hang around humans. As the story goes, once humans started to raise their own food, they could remain in one place for a longer period of time. Canids, such as wolves, jackals, and early domesticated dogs, may all have shared in this new food source from humans. These ancestors to our pets were quick and cunning, and they could spot a good opportunity for an easy meal.

Domestication took place as the tamer canids dined on garbage and scraps, set up house near human settlements, and interbred. These proto-dogs learned to take human handouts as a supplement to their normal diet. Genetic studies suggest that the ancestor of our pets is not in fact the wolf, but a common ancestor of both the wolf and the dog. These carnivores with omnivore tendencies slowly adapted to human food and the human lifestyle, however, the diet of these dog ancestors was largely prey. Studies by Dr. David Mech, and others, show that the wolf's diet is based on large herbivores, but that they also eat smaller mammals, birds, fish, insects, fruit, and plants when they have to. Still, meat, organ meat, fat, and bones are the biggest part of their diet, and were probably the majority of ingredients in the diet of the dog ancestors, as well.

Hints at what this process of domestication may have looked like can be seen today by watching the coyote habitat change. In some cities, packs of coyotes roam urban neighborhoods in search of garbage, cat food, and small domesticated dogs and cats to eat. Lack of prey in the wild, or perhaps the wish for an easier life, has lured coyotes to the urban landscape to supplement their diet.

Picture the same thing happening with the ancestor of our pets 15,000 years ago. Over a long period of time, canids that could coexist with humans produced offspring that grew up with this new social structure. The wary predators morphed into good hunters, protectors, guard dogs, and companions for our villages, homes, and herds. Then, dogs were selected for coat color, type of fur, size, body type, and athletic abilities. These breeds became lovable, beautiful, and skilled.

Our dogs' diets have changed significantly from their ancestors' diet of meat, organs, bones, and a few plants to a diet based on meat and grain by-products.

DOCTOR'S NOTE

Over thousands of years and tens of thousands of generations, genetic changes in the personality and digestive system of the proto-dog occurred. These changes allowed the early dog to adapt to a new carbohydrate-rich diet and an easier lifestyle.

But, unfortunately, as humans bred more and more intensely for color, size, and exaggerated features, many undesirable flaws appeared. The lovable bulldog, once a fit fighter, is now bred for show standards that include a large head, short nose, and low compact body, all without regard to the bulldog's health. Due to AKC (American Kennel Club) standards, the popularity of the breed, and the accompanying overbreeding, they are prone to breathing problems, arthritis, heart problems, and a multitude of skin issues.

Humans favored dogs that would come close, could be trained, and could share our food. That's why our pets can learn to ring a bell by the door to go out and potty. It's also why our dogs tolerate a diet much higher in carbohydrates than their ancestral diet. Stale bread scraps were pretty attractive to a hungry dog, and over thousands of years, a few genetic mutations allowed these newly domesticated animals to digest a food source that we were becoming good at producing—grains. But, even if our dogs are a bit better than their ancestors at digesting grains, we should not forget that, for millions of years, they were adapted to mostly eating high-protein prey.

UNDERSTANDING YOUR DOG'S NUTRITION NEEDS

Historically, dog food was commercially produced to make life easier for the pet owners. Dog biscuits started the cultural shift away from food prepared in the home and were followed by canned food, dry dog meal, and then extruded kibble. Throwaway by-products and carcasses became the basis for commercial food and dog treats. And with cheap grain by-products making up 50 percent, or more, of the food, it was inexpensive to produce and a bargain for pet owners. However, the economical mixes of early dog food did not always have the right balance of ingredients.

A dog's diet should contain a decent level of protein and fat. But is there enough of that in today's commercial dog food? The traditional, economical dog food recipe contains less than 25 percent protein, less than 15 percent fat, and more than 50 percent grain-based carbohydrates, which is not be ideal for every dog. And while some dogs thrive on a medium-protein, low-fat, and high-carbohydrate diet, other dogs need a different recipe. For instance, athletic dogs need more protein, those with a dry coat may need more fat, obese dogs need less fat, and allergic dogs may benefit from less grains. The more you know about your dog's intolerances, the easier it is to choose the best ingredients for their diet.

REGULATING DOG FOOD

How did the regulation and monitoring of dog food production begin? By the 1930s, commercial production of dog food was well underway, and scientists and dog food companies started questioning what necessary nutrients were included in these diets. The U.S. government charged a committee of the National Research Council (NRC) to standardize ingredients in animal food. The NRC's goal was to analyze research data on the effects of feeding purified diets to come up with the level of nutrients needed for health. Once they found out what levels of proteins, fats, vitamins, and minerals were vital, the list was published in 1944. The American Association of Feed Control Officials (AAFCO) took the scientist's list and made it reflect common ingredients that could be economically used in dog food. The list is known as a nutrient profile for dogs. Their European counterpart is the European College of Veterinary Nutrition (ESVN), founded in Vienna in 1991, which oversees that aspect of pet nutrition in Europe. See Resources, page 183, to learn more about these organizations.

It is up to state regulators to compare companies' labels to the nutrient profile and license the sale of the food. The U.S. Food and Drug Administration (FDA) is in charge of regulating pet food safety and inspecting the actual processing. Each state is responsible to make sure that dog food contains the level of nutrients in the nutrient profile provided by the AAFCO—which does not test or enforce any food-related laws.

MAKING SENSE OF NUTRIENT PROFILES

Let's start with the AAFCO nutrient profiles for the average adult dog. In order to better understand the AAFCO nutrient profile. Nutrient profiles list the minimum level of each nutrient in adult dog food in order for the recipe to be "complete and balanced." Your dog or its breed may need more or less protein, fat, carbohydrates, or moisture due to allergies, weight issues, pancreatitis, or urinary problems then is listed in the nutrient profiles. Remember, the AAFCO nutrient profiles are the NRC

DOCTOR'S NOTE

I believe a higher-protein (25 to 30 percent), higher-fat (15 to 20 percent), and lower-carbohydrate (less than 40 percent) diet is the best formula for almost any dog—with the exception of dogs with medical problems, such as pancreatitis, kidney disease, or obesity. Consult your vet to tailor these percentages to your dog's specific needs.

guidelines, derived from purified diets and lab animals, which were then altered to reflect common ingredients in dog food. They are the scientists' educated guess as to what individual nutrients could be added to economical ingredients to keep our dogs healthy.

PROTEIN

Protein is the first nutrient listed in the profile, and it usually comes from meat and the meat by-products. The AAFCO recommends a minimum of 18 percent protein, and that protein should contain the essential amino acids, which are the building blocks of the protein in your dog's body. The essential amino acids are arginine, histidine, isoleucine, leucine, lysine, methionine, phenylalanine, threonine, tryptophan, and valine. Nonessential amino acids cystine and tyrosine reduce the need for essential methionine and phenylalanine, so they are considered equally important. Quality meat, muscle, organ meat, fish, and eggs contain all the essential amino acids needed to keep dogs healthy. Poor-quality pet food may not contain the necessary amino acids.

Depending on activity levels or individual needs, some dogs may need more protein to maintain and repair their protein-dependent muscles, organs, enzymes, and delivery systems. Most commercial dog foods have protein amounts in the 20 to 40 percent range, and hardworking dogs may need the upper part of the range. While the official recommendation is 18 percent protein, I believe our domesticated carnivores deserve a higher amount of protein, above 25 percent, unless your dog has a specific medical condition that requires a lower protein level. Buying a commercial food with better quality protein ingredients or sharing low-fat, healthy protein foods with your dog, such as a few ounces of lean meat, fish, or egg daily, are easy ways to increase the amount of protein in your dog's diet. Plus, those foods have all the essential amino acids your pet needs!

The protein percentage may not mean as much if the protein is not digestible. Chicken eggs, for example, are a wonderful source of protein and are 100 percent digestible, which means the stomach and intestine can break down the protein in the egg and transport the amino acids right through the intestinal cells into the blood. Conversely, the protein in inexpensive meat meal or by-products is not as digestible and may end up on the grass in the backyard. That's what digestibility means—the dog either digests and absorbs it or poops it out.

FAT

Fats are needed for insulation, vitamin storage, cell structure, and fuel. The AAFC's nutrient profile suggests that your dog should have a minimum of 5.5 percent fat. Most dog foods contain more fat, but may not contain the right percentage of *healthy fat*. There are three basic types of

SUGGESTED FAT CONTENT FOR A BALANCED DIET

FAT TYPE	MINIMUM
Crude Fat	5.5%
Essential Fatty Acids (Omega-6 and -3)	
· Linoleic acid	1.1%
· Alpha-linolenic acid (ALA)	0.8%
· Eicosapentaenoic (EPA) + Docosahexaenoic (DHA) acid	0.5%

fats: saturated fats, monounsaturated fatty acids, and polyunsaturated fatty acids. Saturated fats, or stored fuel, is found in large amounts under the skin and in the belly in our domesticated food animals. The healthier monounsaturated fatty acids and polyunsaturated fatty acids are naturally present in muscles, organs, and the bone marrow of all animals. Polyunsaturated fatty acids are a part of all cell membranes and are also necessary to absorb and store important vitamins, such as A, D, and E.

Important classes of polyunsaturated fatty acids are omega 3 and omega 6. Omega-3 and omega-6 fatty acids are important for the brain, the kidneys, joints, skin, and heart function. These essential fatty acids (EFAs) have a role in the inflammatory and anti-inflammatory pathways in the body. Inflammation is important in fighting infection but can damage your dog's irreplaceable organs. The ratio and

levels of essential omega-3 and omega-6 fatty acids are very important in lowering inflammation and protecting the organs of the body. Most commercial foods won't provide the healthful levels of omega-3 and omega-6 needed, so you may want to consider supplements (which will be discussed in detail in chapter 5).

As fat may be troublesome for some dogs, start with small amounts of supplements and increase slowly. My dogs get canned sardines in water or olive oil, canned fish-based dog food, pieces of salmon fillets, and fish oil pills several times a week to make sure they get their anti-inflammatory doses of omega-3s.

The combined doses of DHA and EPA in supplements such as fish oil need to be around 300 mg per 10 pounds (4.5 kg) of the anti-inflammatory fatty acids to be helpful in many medical conditions,

Sardines contain beneficial amounts of omega-3 fatty acids.

DOCTOR'S NOTE

The suggested ratio of omega-6 to omega-3 fatty acids (linoleic + arachidonic acids : ALA + EPA + DHA acids) in the nutrient profile is 30:1. I agree with most human and veterinary nutritionists who suggest less omega-6 and more omega-3 fatty acids in the diet with a ratio of 7:1 or lower. To help balance the ratio of omega-3s to omega-6s, try supplementing with sardines in water or fish oil. Fish or krill oil capsules can also be very effective because fish and krill eat the right diet to be full of these healthful, essential fatty acids.

AAFCO DOG FOOD NUTRIENT PROFILES: MINIMUM VITAMINS AND MINERALS NEEDED

AAFCO's 2014 nutrient profiles for 100 g (about 4 oz) of adult dog food on a dry matter basis. These levels of vitamins and minerals are the minimum needed in 200 g (about 8 oz) of dry food or kibble, or about 400 g (about 16 oz) of moist food (canned or raw food).

MINERAL	MINIMUM	VITAMIN	MINIMUM
Calcium	500mg–1800 mg	Vitamin A	500 IU–25,000 IU
Phosphorus	400mg–1600 mg	Vitamin D	50 IU–300 IU
Calcium-Phosphorous Ratio	1:1–2:1	Vitamin E	5 IU
		Thiamine (B1)	0.23 mg
Potassium	600 mg	Riboflavin (B2)	0.52 mg
Sodium	80 mg	Niacin (B3)	1.36 mg
Chloride	120 mg	Pantothenic acid (B5)	0.12mg
Magnesium	60 mg		
Iron	4 mg	Pyridoxine (B6)	0.15 mg
Copper	0.7 mg	Folic acid (B9)	0.21 mg
Manganese	0.5 mg	Cobalamin (B12)	0.003 mg
Zinc	8 mg	Choline	136 mg
Iodine	0.1 mg–1 mg		
Selenium	0.04 mg–0.2 mg	*IU = international unit*	

Raw, meaty bones are an excellent source of calcium and phosphorus in the correct ratio, but only if your dog is a patient gnawer and not a gulper and swallower.

or 100 mg per 10 pounds of your dog's weight as a daily healthful supplement. In the brand of fish oil pills I use, which are 1,000 mg, the DHA and EPA are listed as 120 mg and 180 mg. So the dose for my little pancreatitis-sensitive dog, Maisy, who weighs 10 pounds, is 300 mg, or one capsule daily for her medical condition, where the average dog may only need a third of that as a daily supplement. You can buy more concentrated versions from your vet, grocery store, vitamin/health food store, or online.

MINERALS

Calcium, phosphorus, potassium, sodium, chloride, magnesium, iron, copper, manganese, zinc, iodine, and selenium are the necessary minerals for bones, muscles, nerves, and enzymes to all function normally. These minerals are part of the building blocks of bone and DNA, they are necessary for muscle contraction or relaxation, and nerves transmit their signals with their help.

Additionally, many proteins, which are enzymes, need a mineral in order to work. For example, the hemoglobin protein wraps around a molecule of iron to attract and carry oxygen around the body. Minerals like sodium, chloride, and potassium help move water in and out of cells, while iodine and the thyroid gland help regulate the rate your dog's body burns energy.

Calcium should always be added to home-cooked dog food unless your dog gets slow-cooked, raw meaty bones to eat. Conversely, overfeeding calcium to pregnant dogs may make their calcium-retrieval system lazy and could cause eclampsia (low calcium and severe tremors) in nursing mothers. Feeding large-breed, growing puppies too much calcium or the wrong calcium/phosphorus ratio can cause poor joint development called "developmental orthopedic disease," which includes hip and elbow dysplasia. (In regular cases, bone meal should be added to home-cooked food at 1 teaspoon (1,300 mg calcium) per pound of meat.)

VITAMINS

The levels of vitamins in AAFCO's nutrient profiles were found to be necessary to keep those vitamin-related processes working. These levels are needed for excellent health, a strong immune system, and cancer prevention. The body needs vitamins to help everything work. Vitamins help create proteins, blood, and bone. They also help your dog absorb nutrients from food. They help the muscles work, fight off aging, and keep nerves and eyesight working. They build DNA and keep blood in the veins by helping blood clot. This chart shows the levels of vitamins needed for an adult dog to prevent deficiencies and illnesses.

Your dog's ancestors got the bulk of their vitamins and minerals from meat, fish, organs, and bone, as well as occasional plants and fruit to round out the diet. Vitamins and minerals may be added to commercial diets, as needed, to balance the amounts in the recipe's ingredients. Vitamin E, an important antioxidant and cancer fighter is often added because it can be low in many processed and home-cooked recipes. Vitamin B12, an essential B vitamin that comes from animals, is commonly supplemented in the diets of dogs that suffer from inflammatory bowel disease (IBD). B12 may not be absorbed very well in these poor, allergic critters and their blood may test low for B12.

KNOWING THE RIGHT LEVELS OF NUTRIENTS

AAFCO nutrient profiles are guides for pet food manufacturers to include the minimal experimental amount of protein, fat, vitamins, and minerals in our dogs' diets to prevent the breakdown of muscles, bone, and organs as well as preclude deficiencies and medical issues. However, these recommended minimum amounts do not always make up the best recipe for health. Remember that a quality mix of ingredients is key to a healthy diet, and we'll explore this in depth throughout the book.

A quick comparison of today's commercial dry food to the nutrient analysis of the ancestral diet (courtesy of the Dog Food Advisor website, dogfoodadvisor.com) suggests that most commercial dry dog food is lower in protein and fat and higher in carbohydrates than the prey-based diet of the dog's ancestors. The moisture content of the ancestral diet may have been in the 50 to 70 percent range, similar to moister diets that serve canned or raw food, dehydrated or freeze-dried food after it is soaked water, and home-prepared food.

NUTRIENT CONTENT COMPARED: ANCESTRAL VS. COMMERCIAL DIET

Today's commercial dog food has less protein and fat and more carbohydrates than what the ancestors of our dogs ate. But why are AAFCO's nutrient profiles so different from the composition of our dog's ancestral diet? Did those ancient canines know something about nutrition and health that our nutritionists and animal scientists have missed?

NUTRIENT	ANCESTRAL DIET	DRY DOG FOOD
Protein	56%	18–32%
Fat	25–30%	8–22%
Carbohydrates	14%	46–74%

DOCTOR'S NOTE

A shift toward the ancestral diet would benefit most dogs and improve the ratio of protein, fat, and carb intake. Adding moisture, protein, and healthy fats can make a diet more similar to our dog's ancestral diet.

Raw diets today are most like the ancestral diet, but they now contain more vegetables and fruit, which put the carbohydrates in the very comfortable 20 to 30 percent range in terms of overall diet composition. Freeze-dried, dehydrated, canned, and home-prepared food also contain more moisture, protein, fat, and fewer carbs than the average dry food and are closer to the time-tested ancestral diet. Dry food is the most popular and convenient food, but no one says it has to be the only food your dog eats.

WHY TODAY'S DIETS INCLUDE SO MANY CARBOHYDRATES

Once the levels of nutrients needed for health were agreed upon, manufacturers could use the least costly ingredients to provide those nutrients listed. Meat by-products—such as fat, organ meats, rice meal, and bone—are readily available and cheap. They can provide the bulk

of the essential nutrients in the profile. When meat by-products are mixed with grain by-products such as cornmeal, corn gluten, wheat gluten, pearled barley, and rice meal, a few extra nutrients, fiber, and volume are gained at a low cost. The goal is to keep the cost down but not to dilute the needed amounts of healthy protein, fat, vitamins, and minerals too much in the recipe. Grain by-products provide a cheap source of energy and fiber and bring the cost of the food way down. That's why the carbohydrate percentage is much higher today than it was in the ancestral diet.

So if grain is good for us, why wouldn't grain by-products be good for our pets? After all, the proto-dog certainly developed the ability to better digest carbohydrates, and our domesticated predators that evolved to eat protein and fat have tolerated the higher amounts of carbohydrates we have served them.

However, today's dog faces high incidences of obesity, diabetes, and cancer. Could these issues be due to more calories, higher fat content, and

DOCTOR'S NOTE

Grain was not present in the diet of the ancestral dog and is a relatively new ingredient in the dog diet. While some dogs do seem to thrive on high levels of grain, it is causing harm to others. As an analogy, think of food as fuel for an engine. Sure, dogs can run on cheaper fuel . . . but is it harming the engine?

more carbs in today's diets? With all the variables, it may be impossible to scientifically prove that the ingredients in today's commercial dog food cause harm, but my experience has been that when dogs are fed moister, higher-protein, and higher-fat choices, many look and feel much better.

So what do we do with this knowledge? How do we get today's diets closer to the ancestral diets? Some may argue that the goal is to feed a higher percentage of protein and fat. If a diet goes up to 25 to 30 percent protein and 15 to 20 percent fat, that will decrease the carbs to somewhere in the 40 percent range, a bit nearer the ancestral number. We'll talk about the merits of the different types of foods and how you can use them to bump up the moisture, protein, and fat, while lowering the carbs. Additionally, you can accomplish these results without having to go to an entirely new diet. You can feed your dog less dry food by adding in a bit of canned food or water or chicken broth

to kibble. You can even throw in a couple ounces of lean chicken, beef, pork, or fish several times a week to raise the levels of protein and fat. Whatever your approach, never raise the amount of fat suddenly or change the type of animal protein dramatically in fat-sensitive or allergic dogs. However, dogs that are fat sensitive can still enjoy a piece of lean meat or fish a couple times a week.

There are a lot of factors when it comes to determining the proper diet for your dog— breed, size, age, allergies, sensitivities, and illnesses chief among them. It may take time, effort, and patience to find the right diet for your dog. As you probably know by now, there is no one answer that will suit all dogs. Read on for more ways to choose the right food for your dog, based on his specific dietary needs.

KEY POINTS

1. Our dogs evolved from predators that ate meat, organs, and a small variety of other available food sources. Once they depended on us for food, their diet drastically changed. From the balance of nutrients in prey animals, to a mix of meat and grain by-products, researchers determined the amount of nutrients in the diet needed for health.

2. Nutrient profiles should not be taken as dietary advice. Scientists used purified diets in laboratory feeding trials to determine the nutrients necessary for survival and health. AAFCO's nutrient profiles adopted and refined those studies to reflect common, economical ingredients for dog food. Each commercial dog food may be complying with those minimal levels of nutrients in nutrient profiles, but they do not always address an individual dog's needs.

3. Each of our dogs may have different needs. Their ancestors ate a mix of quality muscle, healthy fat, and organ meat that included the right amount of protein, fat, omega fatty acids, calcium phosphorous, iron, and other vitamins and minerals. When we try to make commercial food cost-effective and convenient, the ingredients will ultimately make it a healthy choice (or not).

The Alaskan Malamute has a powerful, sturdy body made for perseverance and strength. Discuss with your veterinarian the level of protein and fat necessary for this breed to maintain his active profile.

CHAPTER 2

FINDING THE RIGHT DOG FOOD FOR YOUR DOG

MOST PEOPLE THINK THAT DOG FOODS MADE BY SMALLER COMPANIES ARE A BETTER CHOICE THAN THOSE FROM LARGER, WELL-KNOWN COMPANIES.

Dog Food Advisor suggests, however, that smaller, lesser-known companies aren't always the best choice. In fact, 73 of the 88 recall events documented on their website during a recent five-year period were linked to products from smaller brands. Even though smaller companies account for just 7 percent of the pet food and treats sold in North America, they were responsible for 83 percent of the recalls.

In addition, after conducting hundreds of interviews, Dog Food Advisor concluded that a significant number of dog foods from smaller brands are not likely to meet the claims of nutritional adequacy printed on their labels. They added that many smaller companies willingly admitted that they make no effort to verify the nutrient content or the safety of the foods they sell. They concluded that the smaller the brand, the less likely the company has the financial ability to perform all the steps needed to ensure the quality of its products.

Pet food is a big business owned by huge conglomerates. Although there are always exceptions, it's important to keep in mind that larger companies are far more likely to employ food scientists, animal nutritionists, and other veterinary professionals to design their products, test raw materials for nutrients and contaminants, have quality control, and own manufacturing facilities and testing facilities. On the other hand, the ingredients chosen by huge conglomerates may be based on cost rather than quality, as the corporations reach out for the best global deal.

I have always recommended and bought higher quality, well-known brands from midsize companies and stayed away from the economical offerings of the largest pet food manufacturers. The ingredient lists of the huge companies usually contain more highly processed by-products, synthetic ingredients, and unnecessary chemicals and dyes.

Choosing the right brand of pet food depends on a number of factors. Some people are tempted to think smaller, boutique brands are better, but, in fact, such brands are responsible for the majority of recalls in North America.

Most people don't have the time or desire to research every available dog food brand, especially considering all of the behind-the-scenes swaps happening in brand ingredients. There are kibble diets, moist diets, semimoist diets, refrigerated chub diets, canned foods, dehydrated foods, freeze-dried foods, raw foods, grain-free foods, joint diets, weight-loss diets, breed-specific diets, puppy diets, limited-ingredient diets, and prescription diets. Even we veterinarians, with years of experience with a variety of diets, are blown away when we enter a pet store and see the sheer volume of products with their different shapes, sizes, and vibrant packaging.

The best food for an individual dog depends on the pet's needs and the owner's budget. The diet may need to help out with medical problems such as skin problems, ear problems, obesity, gastrointestinal problems, bladder issues, diabetes, or seizures. Although a better-quality food can seem expensive, it can also help offset the high cost of repeated visits to a veterinary clinic. If a better diet minimizes or prevents costly medical problems, then that diet makes sense economically as well as medically. However, the right ingredients at the right price don't always guarantee success. The chosen diet has to then pass the smell and taste test from the dog. Some dogs are picky and won't tolerate certain meats, carbs, or the different ways the food is made. That's where the owner's persistence and patience comes in. It may take a few different food choices before you find the right food for you and your dog.

As you cruise the pet food aisles, you'll see lots of bags of dry food, but less canned food, and even less of the other types of dog food (raw, freeze-dried raw, dehydrated, cooked, and refrigerated). Dry food outsells canned food by about four times. According to the Pet Food Institute, a U.S. trade association representing dog food manufacturers, sales of dry dog food were about 9 billion dollars compared to 2.3 billion for the canned dog food. Their

DOCTOR'S NOTE

I recommend buying dog food containing excellent ingredients from well-known, midsize companies over enormous conglomerates whose decisions about ingredients are more likely to be cost driven.

data, published in 2012, also indicate that sales of foods other than dry or canned amounted to only 5 percent of pet food sales. Sales of raw food are slowly growing despite getting the thumbs down by most vets and their professional association, the American Veterinary Medical Association (AVMA). Increased sales are likely due to the natural and organic trends in human and canine nutrition. Raw food is less processed, more natural, and more similar to the ancestral diet of our dogs, and as the popularity of ancestral human diets increase (e.g., the paleo diet), so do those of the dog. For additional information see the World Small Animal Veterinary Association (WSAVA) website—a global veterinary initiative focusing on animal wellness and nutrition. See Resources, page 183.

UNDERSTANDING DRY AND CANNED FOODS

The popularity of foods dictates how stores stock the shelves. Dry food will be most evident, followed by canned food, and then the other types. It's important to remember that the most popular food is not necessarily the best type of food for all dogs. Dry food is the most popular because it is the easiest and most economical to feed.

Your brand of dry dog food depends on your budget and your dog's needs. Blue Buffalo, Taste of the Wild, Natural Balance, and Nature's Domain (the Kirkland brand of Taste of the Wild), Orijen, and Acana are good quality choices for dry dog food at a good price. The best dry dog foods, in general, share a few things in common. First, the food's sources of protein will be listed by specific animal used, instead of saying meat meal, animal fat, or animal by-products. Second, the list of ingredients won't display controversial synthetic preservatives or humectants such as BHA, BHT, TBHQ, Ethoxyquin, or propylene glycol. Third, they won't contain wheat gluten or other grain by-products, but will list vegetables, fruit, or whole nongluten grains. Finally, the protein percentage will be around 25 to 30 percent and the fat percentage will be in the 15 to 20 percent range.

If most dogs thrive on a quality dry food, why wouldn't you feed dry dog food alone? Here are several possible reasons you would add in another type of food:

1. You may want to feed a moister food with lower carbohydrates and fewer preservatives, which is closer to the ancestral diet. Such food includes canned, semimoist, refrigerated, raw, home-cooked food, or a combination of any or all of these.

2. Your dog is prone to Gastric Dilation Volvulus (or bloat). A mix of dry and moist food (or table scraps) is better than either alone.

Canned food is the subject of many myths, but if you buy a high-quality brand with ingredients your dog can tolerate, it can be the basis of a healthy diet.

3. Your dog is prone to obesity and even the low-fat dry foods don't decrease its weight. Canned food or other moister, higher-protein, medium-fat, and lower-carb foods may help your dog shed unneeded pounds.

4. Your dog is prone to form urinary crystals and bladder stones. Moister food such as canned homemade or moist raw food is needed to prevent them. Dry or canned prescription diets may also be necessary.

5. Your dog has dry skin, skin or ear allergies, or a sensitive gut. These conditions often don't improve in a dog that solely eats dry food. Skin, ear, and gut sensitivities usually stem from ingredients such as wheat gluten, beef, chicken, dairy, or other allergens. Some dogs with chronic medical issues really improve when canned food, raw food, or homemade food is used instead of dry food.

Should you consider feeding canned food or mixing it in with dry food? Canned food was popular until dry food began production in the 1950s. Since then, it has been ranked the second most popular choice. It is a bit more expensive, has more of an odor, and suffers from a couple of common dog food myths.

Canned Food Myth 1: Canned food contains undesirable ingredients and will cause diarrhea or loose stools.

It is true that the cheaper canned foods often contain beef by-products, beef fat, and wheat gluten. For sensitive dogs, that recipe is sure to cause soft stools because those ingredients are the worst offenders in stomach and bowel issues. If a dog gets diarrhea from eating canned food, it is not caused by the increased moisture but by the presence of allergens, higher fat, or gluten. But if you know what to look for, there are many quality canned food products out there with great ingredients.

 ## DOCTOR'S NOTE

Canned food usually has fewer calories per ounce, more oils, and less irritating ingredients and may be ideal for overweight dogs, dogs with moderate-to-severe allergies, or dogs with a dry coat.

Canned Food Myth 2: Canned food doesn't help keep a dog's teeth clean.

The truth is that most dogs inhale their food without the chewing action required to clean teeth. Therefore, neither canned nor dry food help clean the teeth. In reality, the cause of tartar is linked more to genetics and the breed of dog than the type of food eaten.

I recommend canned food more than dry food because canned usually has fewer calories per ounce, a higher percentage of fat, fewer preservatives, more moisture to aid in digestion, and canning helps preserve the food and prevent oxidation of the fat and vitamin E.

Cheaper dry and canned foods may bathe a dog's cells and organs in unnecessary chemicals, such as synthetic preservatives, food colors, or other processing additives. Many chronic medical conditions are idiopathic, which means "cause unknown." They are caused by inflammation of the organs such as the skin, ears, kidneys, liver, and intestines. I've found that many idiopathic chronic medical conditions may respond to different ingredients or fewer irritating ingredients in the diet.

HOW COMMERCIAL DOG FOOD IS MADE

Kibble is made by mixing together all the ingredients to form a moist dough that is then fed into an extruder, which cooks it under intense heat and pressure and forms the pieces. Once it passes out of the extruder, it expands in the open air, is dried in an oven, cooled, and packaged.

Canned food is made by combining all the ingredients in a mixer, then doled out into cans and sealed. The cans are then cooked, cooled, and labeled.

Raw foods have a mix of natural, balanced, beneficial nutrients. Consider offering your pup raw food as a nutritious treat.

DOCTOR'S NOTE

Commercial raw diets are becoming more popular as people look for healthy ingredients, fewer gluten grains, and fewer synthetic preservatives. I believe raw food can be an important part of any dog's diet, but it must be introduced gradually.

REFRIGERATED COOKED FOOD AND RAW FOOD

The refrigerated/frozen section of a pet store houses cooked and raw foods. Cooked foods called "chubs," are refrigerated rolled foods that look like thick sausages. They often contain quality ingredients (similar to high-quality canned foods) and natural preservatives. There are several other types of cooked foods available now, and this area appears to be growing. Most raw foods use a mix of meat and organs, bones, and carbohydrates from veggies or fruit. The ingredients are ground and shaped into chubs, patties, or bites that are then thawed before feeding. One type of raw food may have a simple raw-chicken ingredient list—60 percent chicken meat, 30 percent organ meat (liver and gizzard), and 10 percent ground bone—and use no heat processing, no synthetic vitamins, and no pressure processing. Others are more involved. Nature's Variety Instinct

blend, for example, has chicken (including ground chicken bone), turkey heart, turkey liver, turkey bone, yeast culture, pumpkin seeds, montmorillonite clay, apples, broccoli, butternut squash, salt, cod liver oil, dried kelp, carrots, spinach, dried chicory root, and blueberries.

The healthy combination of ingredients in raw food decreases the need for synthetic vitamins or other minerals, and because the food is kept refrigerated or frozen, it needs fewer preservatives. Raw food is usually gluten free with more protein and fat than other types of food. It can help clear the skin and make a shiny coat. However, it is made up of raw meat (beef or chicken), fat, or organs, which some dogs cannot tolerate.

As I mentioned, raw foods can be purchased frozen, dehydrated, air dried, and freeze dried. All kinds contain quality ingredients and natural preservatives, but have varying degrees of rawness. Dehydrated and air-dried dog food has had the moisture removed from the raw meat and veggies using the circulation of heated air (under 200°F, (93°C)) around the ingredients. Because the processing is so mild, dehydrated and air-dried food is still considered to be "raw."

A newer, more convenient type of raw food is called freeze-dried raw food. Freeze-drying uses low temperatures and low pressure to remove the water without that moisture going to a solid ice phase. The ground meat, bones, and carbs are left untouched by the ice, as the water goes right from liquid to gas and floats away. The ingredients transition from raw to freeze dried without ever being thawed or cooked, thereby retaining all of the nutritional value of raw meat.

Raw food manufacturers must address the safety concerns of raw food's potential for contamination. The Honest Kitchen gently steams meat, fish, and leafy greens to remove pathogens before dehydrating all the ingredients. Stella & Chewy's uses hydrostatic high pressure (pasteurization) to eliminate harmful bacteria in the ingredients, and an independent lab tests every batch for dangerous bacterial pathogens such as *E. coli* and salmonella.

Depending on a dog's tolerance to the type of animal protein in the mix and to fat, a raw diet may be a good choice. You can use raw, dehydrated, or freeze-dried products in combination with other foods, or as a very nutritious treat. It's an easy way to bump up the protein level and quality of the ingredients in your dog's diet. Transitioning a dog to a raw-food diet may involve trying different raw diets and different animal proteins, or a diet with a lower percentage of fat. It may take a few weeks for the gut to get used to the intestinal and bacterial changes that occur. The higher fat content found in these raw foods can cause diarrhea and pancreas inflammation in sensitive dogs or kibble-raised dogs. If your dog falls into any of these categories, it may benefit from a very slow transition, which can be aided by mixing a small amount of the new food mixed into their normal diet for several weeks' time. Be aware that the high amount of fat may lead to obesity in less active dogs.

Please note that your veterinarian may not fully endorse the raw-food diet. The American Veterinary Medical Association's (AVMA) official statement on the matter warns dog owners of the dangers of pathogens that may not be fully eliminated in raw food because it has not been cooked to a high temperature. The AVMA does not yet endorse alternative methods for eliminating pathogens, such as Salmonella and *E. coli*, and pets may (rarely) contract food-borne illness and, in some cases, transmit pathogens to their human owners.

Home cooking for your dog gives you total control of the ingredients that make up his diet.

A raw diet has a number of nutritional benefits, but most dogs need time to adjust to the higher fat content, and some can't tolerate it at all.

The dangers of feeding raw food are often lumped together with complications of eating raw meaty bones (or RMBs). This is a practice that can lead to broken teeth, choking, and intestinal obstructions, if the size of the bones and the eating or chewing style of the dog are not taken into account. Eating or breaking off large pieces of RMBs can lead to problems, while contentedly gnawing on appropriately sized pieces of raw bones will clean the teeth and provide a great source of joint nutrition and balanced minerals (calcium, phosphorus, and magnesium). Frozen, raw chicken necks and wings are other examples of raw food that are very nutritious and may also help rid the teeth of tartar. And as long as you feed them frozen or just thawed in the microwave (be careful, as the center gets hot quickly), the bacteria doesn't have time to incubate and cause issues. You can research global nutrition guidelines on the WSAVA website. For contact information, see Resources, page 183.

I feel comfortable feeding different types of raw foods to my own pets and think that it is a safe and nutritious way to feed your dog, even though raw foods have a small risk of health concerns for humans and dogs due to bacterial contamination. I feed raw food as 10 percent of my dog's diet, as I prefer to feed my dogs a mix of canned, home-cooked, dehydrated, and raw foods. You have to weigh the potential risks of bacterial contamination and infection from feeding raw foods for yourself and decide what is right for you and your pet.

VETERINARY PRESCRIPTION FOODS

Prescription diets are formulated with ingredients to help with medical conditions, such as bladder stones, diabetes, liver problems, allergies, or pancreatitis. One such prescription diet, Hill's Prescription Diet k/d Canine Renal Health, was designed by Dr. Mark Morris Sr., D.V.M, for dogs with kidney failure and modeled on recipes recommended for human kidney-failure patients. The k/d sold today lists the ingredients as water, egg white, cornstarch, pork liver, chicken fat (preserved with mixed tocopherols and citric acid), sucrose, flaxseed, and dried whey. This mix has a lower amount of protein and phosphorus, which has been traditionally thought to extend the life of failing kidneys. But while the nutrients contained in the recipe will aid the failing kidneys, the lack of healthful oils or a sensitivity to other ingredients in the diet may lead to other medical problems such as dry or itchy skin.

The timing of putting dogs on lifelong prescription diets is also debated. Some researchers feel that early signs of kidney and liver problems are better served with higher-quality protein ingredients instead of immediately opting for a lower-protein diet. The latest research questions the need for liver and kidney diets in very early stages of liver and kidney dysfunction. In some cases, a high-quality senior diet may also help dogs with early signs of liver or kidney issues. When those organs are moderately or severely compromised, a prescription diet may be helpful but not necessarily before.

Fortunately, high-quality, limited-ingredient diets and senior diets have reduced the need for higher-priced intestinal diets and prescription diets for food allergies. When itchy skin and red ears don't respond to commercial limited-ingredient diets, then prescription, limited-ingredient diets, hydrolyzed chicken, or soy diets by brands such as Hills, Royal Canin, and Purina may be more helpful. (Protein is the nutrient that causes allergic reactions, and in hydrolyzed diets the protein is enzymatically digested into very small amino acid units that aren't recognized as allergens

Prescription diets such as Royal Canin S/O may also be needed for dogs that form struvite or oxalate urinary crystals or bladder stones, and it may be one of the only nutritional therapies that will help. Struvite and oxalate bladder stones *may*

be prevented with a moister (canned, raw, homemade) diet that is supplemented with cranberry extract and potassium citrate. Prevention of urate stones, however, usually requires daily medication (allopurinol) and a prescription diet, such as Hill's Prescription Diet u/d Canine Non-Struvite Urinary Tract Health.

Joint-formula prescription diets may have fewer calories with added glucosamine/chondroitin, and fish oil. Offering glucosamine/chondroitin, fish oil capsules, or sardines as a supplement assures that the joint nutrition and omega fatty acids are present in both the quantity and quality needed, instead of relying on the prescription diet alone.

Low-fat prescription diets such as Royal Canin Gastrointestinal Low-Fat Diet control the symptoms of pancreatitis. This prescription diet works well except when patients are gluten sensitive, as the dry food contains wheat and barley. A low-fat senior diet instead of a prescription diet may also be helpful to dogs sensitive to fat. Aim for 2 to 3% fat in canned food and 10% in the dry food.

The real problem with many prescription diets is that many dogs don't enjoy the lack of flavor, so their owners feed them treats or foods to improve the flavor. The ingredients in these treats, however, dilute and pollute the beneficial ones

Some dogs, particularly older ones, can benefit from prescription diets that can treat a variety of health problems, ranging from arthritis to bladder stones.

and negate the value of the prescription diet. If you have to trick your dog with alternate flavors and treats, consider healthy options. For example, low-fat flavor enhancers such as a small amount of chicken broth, sardines, or lean meat may trick that nose and entice the chubby dog to eat the prescription diet or special diet it is supposed to eat.

HOME-COOKED DIETS

Home-prepared diets are often maligned and held suspect by the veterinary and commercial pet-food folks. The cry of unbalanced pet foods and deficiencies scares many dog owners and can steer them away from home-prepared dog food or even sharing human food. I, too, was a bit nervous when I started cooking for my own fur babies. However, after many years of observing the effects of home cooking, I've found that some dogs' skin, ear, and gut issues resolve when healthy human-food ingredients are used in home-cooked dog food, and many of my clients have had the same results.

Home cooking can provide quality ingredients with no preservatives at less cost than commercial dog food. And some people enjoy sharing healthy food and cooking for their pets. If dog owners have the time and don't mind, why shouldn't they? It makes them feel good, saves some money, and is good for their dogs. When you home cook, you can decide what quality of ingredients you want to feed your dog. If you want free-range, organic, or grass-fed meat, you can buy those more expensive ingredients and serve them to your dog. If you want to home prepare a limited-ingredient diet for your picky-eater pup, start with a single protein or mix a protein and carbohydrate. It's up to you.

And remember, it doesn't have to be all or nothing. Some owners offer only home-prepared food to their dogs, while others add the home-cooked food to commercial dry or wet food. Note that, just as in starting with any new food, each dog reacts differently to the varying ingredients, and each dog transitions at his own pace to the new diet.

There are some guidelines you should follow when prepping a home-cooked meal to provide your dog complete nutrition. Home-prepared foods need to contain meat, organs, eggs, fish, and a variety of carbohydrates. Dogs also need a daily source of calcium in their diet, which may come from raw meaty bones, softened cooked bones, or calcium supplements such as bone meal. If you do not feel comfortable feeding a diet that has not had a nutritional analysis, you can add a vitamin/mineral supplement or consult with a veterinary nutritionist about a balanced, home-prepared diet. We'll talk more about home cooking and recipes in chapter 3.

Many people are wary of feeding their dog home-cooked diets, but if you understand ingredients, homemade food can clear up some chronic skin and gut issues.

Different dogs have different needs, and it may take some patience and experimentation to find the right diet for your dog.

KEY POINTS

1. When choosing food for your dog, remember that the majority of foods in pet stores reflect their popularity and convenience. Many pet foods in the supermarket or pet store are manufactured by huge companies that may use economical or poor-quality ingredients. These marginal ingredients may fit the canine nutrient profile but contain less-desirable ingredients that may not be great for your dog.

2. The ancestral diet contained more protein and fat, and many of today's dogs will look and feel better with a little more of both in their diet.

3. If your dog seems happier and healthier with a higher-quality or less-processed food, regardless of cost, that food is a better choice. If you opt for dry food, whether it is for ease or cost, consider buying food that is gluten-free with quality ingredients and a decent protein and fat percentage, as discussed on page 34.

4. Your dog may require a hypoallergenic or limited-ingredient diet. Common allergens include wheat, beef, chicken and dairy. I've also found that dogs can be irritated by unlisted or even uncommon ingredients. It may take trial and error with a very restricted diet to find the particular foods with the fewest ingredients that help the most.

5. Finding the right diet is a personal process. Many smaller dog-food companies and advisors (like Dog Food Advisor) have changed the way we shop and buy dog food. We are no longer prisoners of the foods recommended by vets, advertised on TV, or available in grocery stores. Your vet may or may not be able to help you decide between the many different diets available today, but, if you are careful with transitions and focus on ingredients or previous medical issues, different types of diets can make a big difference in your dog's health.

CHAPTER 3
FEEDING HEALTHY HUMAN FOOD
AND AVOIDING TOXIC FOOD

DOES YOUR DOG CONSTANTLY DINE WITH YOU, OR DO YOU SHARE ONLY AN OCCASIONAL BITE? MANY PEOPLE ARE AFRAID TO ADMIT THEY SHARE FOOD WITH THEIR DOGS. WHY DO VETS AND COMMERCIAL DOG FOOD COMPANIES DISCOURAGE SHARING FOOD WITH OUR PETS?

Table scraps developed a bad reputation because solely feeding meat and bone scraps have the potential for harm. For example, feeding an all-meat-scrap diet to nursing dogs and growing puppies has caused medical issues and growth problems. An all-meat diet without bones doesn't have enough calcium to balance out the phosphorus in the meat. Feeding a fatty piece of meat to any dog that is prone to pancreatitis could send its pancreas into orbit. Sharing steak bones, drumsticks, or ribs can lead to problems when large or sharp pieces are swallowed and require surgery to remove. And fatty meat or cooked bones may cause dogs to get sick, vomit, have diarrhea, have severe constipation, or even develop an intestinal obstruction. Knowing that, you can see how scraps got such a bad reputation.

Nobody wants to feed their dog something that will make it sick, but table scraps don't need to cause sickness, discomfort, or diarrhea as long as you know what foods are safe. The term "table scraps" came from our practice of giving our dogs the part of the meal we did not want. More often than not, the term used to mean a fatty piece of meat, but the definition has changed as much as the dog's status in our families. Due to the healthier direction of human nutrition, table scraps are much higher quality now than in the past. In fact, "healthy human food" is a better description of the variety of healthy foods pet owners are willing to share with their furry families.

"I don't feed my dog any human food" is a common answer to my questions about recent treats that may have caused a patient's nausea and diarrhea. In reality, my question is about any new biscuits or treats. Gluten-filled biscuits are more apt to cause diarrhea than some healthy human food. Despite that, veterinarians and the pet food industry usually advise against supplementing a diet with human food. The common mythology or advice from a friend, relative, breeder, veterinarian, or Google may warn you about destroying the "complete and balanced" nutrition of a commercial diet by feeding table scraps.

Veterinarians' real worry is that people will feed their dogs a large portion of foods they are not accustomed to or give sensitive dogs a meat or fatty meal they can't tolerate—not that owners will disrupt "complete and balanced" nutrition. We are also concerned when obese dogs are fed too many calories and when owners share unhealthy foods such as pastries, ice cream, or dangerous cooked bones. Sharing healthy human food will not cause any nutritional imbalances or medical issues in dogs, as long as you test small amounts of the food first to see how your dog reacts and vary ingredients accordingly.

Here is a good rule of thumb to follow: treats should not comprise more than 10 percent of the diet. However, if the treats are healthy human food instead of the calorie-laden, vitamin-deficient, cheap biscuits and chews, they can be more than 10 percent. Healthy proteins, fats, and a variety of vegetables can add value to a dog's diet. (By the way, not all treats and chews are nutritionally bankrupt. In the last few years, an explosion of healthy treats and chews has become available.)

FEEDING WITH CAUTION

If your dog has medical problems or sensitivities, then you may have to watch the level of fat, protein, carbohydrates, or glutens in the healthy human food or treats you share with them. Dogs prone to obesity or pancreatitis don't need the extra fat. Dogs with failing kidneys don't need extra protein in the diet. Diabetics don't need extra carbs such as starchy or sugary food. Dogs with skin, ear, or gut problems may be sensitive to beef, wheat, chicken, dairy, or soy products. A

kibble-reared dog with an easily upset stomach or bowels may be overwhelmed by fatty beef; the stomach and bowel simply cannot handle the different meat and fat. Some of the fat is digested and absorbed, but the rest may exit in an ugly way. Diarrhea that is brownish-red and textured like jelly or pudding, or stool that contains drops of red blood, are sure signs of intestinal disturbance and angry colon. If this occurs, dogs should fast for 12 hours and then eat a meal or two of white rice and chicken broth or chicken baby food, and/or low-fat cottage cheese and probiotics to help the bowel recover. However, illness and severe diarrhea always warrants a veterinary visit.

Avoid giving your dog a whole bowl of food that it is not accustomed to eating. That is the recipe for stomach upset and diarrhea. Can you imagine how you would feel if you ate a big steak after living on a steady diet of oat flakes your whole life? It will take some time for you to see what foods your dog likes and which foods agree with it. The secret is to share small amounts of different kinds of meats or fish, rice, potatoes, or vegetables, until you know which foods they can handle without problems. Over time, my experience has been that most dogs will adapt to the variety of their new diet.

SAFE AND HEALTHY HUMAN FOOD

I've spent many years learning about food ingredients and how to safely share

THE DOWNSIDE OF TABLE FOOD

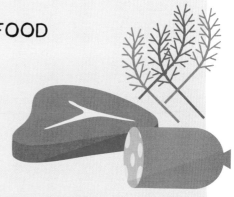

Feeding scraps from the table will encourage a dog to beg, jump up, and get up on the back of the couch, stare, and whimper. Many pet owners don't want their dogs to behave this way. Other owners love to share and encourage begging. It just depends on whether you find that type of behavior annoying or endearing. No matter which side of the fence you are on, you can still safely share healthy food from your table to supplement a dog's diet. To avoid a dog's begging, try adding healthy human food directly to his usual food, or, if there is a good portion of it, it can be a complete meal.

human food with our dogs. I enjoy the stories of what foods dogs decide to eat. Some dogs love tomatoes, while others break out in hives after eating them. Mini carrots are a great low-calorie treat that some dogs like, while other dogs will leave them lying on the floor and look at you quizzically. My Lab, Tucker, used to love carrots and apples. My golden, Teddy, used to wait for tomatoes to ripen to pull them from the garden like a tasty red ball. My terrier cross, Maisy, wasn't interested in canned green beans or fresh green beans from the market, but would pull the sweet, young green beans fresh off the vine. Clients have entertained me with stories

of dogs eating cantaloupe, peaches, and watermelon.

Check out the labels of natural or higher-quality commercial food for inspiration. Years ago, when I became convinced that feeding a better diet was important, I started feeding my dogs a different brand. The label read like a shopping list of safe food ingredients for dogs: chicken, eggs, pea protein, oats, vegetable broth, pearled barley, chicken fat, whole peas, chicken liver, salmon, flaxseed, salmon oil, pea fiber, sweet potatoes, apples, blueberries, green beans, carrots, cranberries, zucchini, and alfalfa. Such labels offer great ideas for safe foods to share.

Teach your pup early that human food is not for him and stick to the message. You'll be glad later when he's fully grown and might be more determined to share your meal or snack.

If your dog is already used to a varied diet and has never experienced nausea, vomiting, or bouts of soft stool or diarrhea, then you may be able to offer meat, veggies, and rice to him all at once. It is always more prudent to try one type of lean meat in combination with a bland carbohydrate, such as potatoes or rice, if your dog has a sensitive stomach or bowel. If you have found that your dog is intolerant of beef or chicken ingredients in commercial food, then you also need to avoid sharing those ingredients with him in the form of food scraps. Sensitive pets may enjoy a bit of lean pork, fish, rice, potatoes, and peas with carrots.

For particularly spicy or salty human foods, or foods with garlic or onion bases, I tend to rinse them first before sharing. Don't worry about a small amount of onions or garlic in the meat or veggies— it takes a few ounces of onion or several garlic cloves daily to make the average medium-size dog suffer from a type of anemia caused by sulfides in the onions or garlic associated with these foods.

TABLE SCRAPS TO AVOID

The most important thing in feeding healthy human food to dogs is to make sure the food does not include cooked bones. Generally, almost every time a dog does snag a chicken bone, steak bone, or rib bone from an abandoned plate or unattended garbage bag, the bone passes through the body uneventfully. Depending on the amount of bones eaten, the poop may change color, lighten up, or even look like white chalk. However, if a large quantity (a turkey carcass, for example), big pieces, or sharp pieces of bone are swallowed, medical problems can occur.

Constipation from bones is much more common than a blockage, and an intestinal puncture by a sharp piece of bone is rare. Constipation can result from bone sediment and fragments piling up in the colon and slowing passage. The longer the bone loiters, the harder and drier it

gets. In this case, your dog may appear pained or strain when it attempts to poop. Laxatives and enemas may be necessary to break up the bone pile.

The most dangerous event occurs when greedy dogs hurriedly chomp on cooked steak bones or chicken bones. Instead of carefully gnawing them, they break the bones into large or sharp pieces and swallow them. A sharp piece may pierce any part of the digestive tract or come to a complete stop about halfway through the longest part of the small intestine. A large, cooked-bone blockage or a sharp, cooked-bone penetration requires surgery and can be very dangerous. A dog who feels sick, vomits, and bloats after eating bones may signal problems and the need for a checkup. If a dog looks happy and continues to eat and poop, however, it'll be fine.

Eating big, hard, baked bones or cooked bones can also fracture a dog's shearing premolars. In other words, in the rush to down the bony delicacy, a greedy dog may crack its teeth.

On the other hand, feeding dogs raw, small bones or very large, raw beef bones can be a safe practice, depending on your dog's style of chewing. Happy, contented gnawing on raw big bones and careful chewing of smaller, raw bones are the chewing styles suited for raw meaty bones. An anxious, hurried eater that starts mouthing and cracking large raw bones can run into the same problems as

Table scraps such as barbecued or baked bones (see page 55) and fatty meat can be harmful to your dog, but that doesn't mean all human food is off limits.

one who eats cooked or baked bones. If your dog is a hurried, greedy eater, then raw bones are not for him.

In general, baked goods and desserts have high carbohydrate content and low amounts of protein, vitamins, and minerals. In addition to the sugar found in these items, baked goods contain wheat flour, which can cause gluten-sensitive dogs to itch/vomit or squirt.

If your dog is heavy, green vegetables or small pieces of lean meat are good choices. Proteins satisfy hunger more than carbohydrates, but avoid fatty meat because it has more calories. If you do share some lean meat with your weight-challenged dog, just cut back on the dog food or skip that night's meal. Low-calorie vegetables, such as carrots and green beans, sometimes make great treats or can be served with low-fat broth as a low-calorie meal. We'll mention these tactics again later when we talk about dog obesity (see chapter 8).

If you want to discourage begging, you should feed your dog human food mixed with dog food only in her dog bowl—never directly from the table.

SOME HEALTHY FOODS YOU *CAN* SHARE WITH YOUR PET

The following is a list of foods I commonly feed my pets. It is not a comprehensive list, but it can be used as a foundation.

✓ **PROTEINS:** Chicken, chicken liver, deli turkey slices, pork, salmon fillets (no whole raw salmon or trout), tilapia, canned sardines, shrimp, shrimp tails, eggs, beef, beef liver, lamb, venison, elk. (Always start with lean meat, and be aware that beef and chicken are common allergenic meats.)

✓ **NUTS:** Peanuts, walnuts, almonds

✓ **DAIRY:** Cottage cheese, cheese, yogurt. (Note that some dogs are intolerant of dairy products.)

✓ **FATS:** Fish oil, olive oil, coconut oil, canola oil

✓ **VEGETABLES, STARCHES, CARBOHYDRATES:** Green beans, peas, carrots, squash, broccoli (small amounts), kale, tomatoes, tomato sauce, potatoes, sweet potatoes, quinoa, rice, gluten-free pasta, garbanzo beans, lentils, oatmeal.

✓ **FRUIT:** Apples, bananas, cantaloupe, peaches, strawberries, blueberries

FOODS TO AVOID FEEDING TO YOUR PET

The foods below are generally to be avoided. Many are toxic to dogs per the ASPCA Poison Control Center. Others are to be fed with caution and/or in moderation, if at all.

 CHOCOLATE, COFFEE, CAFFEINE: These contain caffeine like chemicals that can cause vomiting, diarrhea, panting, hyperactivity, heart problems, tremors, seizures, or death. Chocolate gets the most attention because most people don't take their pets out for an espresso. Baking chocolate and dark chocolate are the most toxic. Toxic doses of theobromine, the chemical troublemaker, are 9 mg per pound of dog for mild signs, up to 18 mg per pound of dog for severe signs. Milk chocolate contains 44 mg per ounce of theobromine, while semisweet chocolate contains 150 mg per ounce, and baking chocolate contains 390 mg per ounce. Many people rush to the veterinary emergency room after their medium-to-large dog eats a square of milk chocolate, which is usually not necessary. In the case of larger amounts of chocolate, especially dark chocolate, however, you should head to the vet ER or induce vomiting immediately, because the chocolate is easily and rapidly absorbed. If the evidence points to a small amount of milk chocolate or the crime involves other chocolate and a large dog, you may try to figure out how much chocolate was eaten before you rush off to the ER. You can check out chocolate toxicity calculators online: www.petmd.com/dog/chocolate-toxicity.

 ## DOCTOR'S NOTE

Milk chocolate contains one tenth of the toxic theobromine as dark chocolate. A small amount of milk chocolate will not cause symptoms in a medium to large dog. When concerned, head to the vet ER, but you may want to check out the chocolate toxicity calculators online.

ALCOHOL: Most dogs don't like the taste of it and would not drink enough to harm themselves. So a taste of beer, wine, or margarita won't hurt your dog. However, if a dog went after it, too much might cause problems for a dog that was sensitive to the effects of alcohol. My nephew's dog, Pepper, always enjoyed a shot of tequila and a nap. I do not condone it, but I have learned to stay out of arguments with family members.

 MACADAMIA NUTS: Macadamia nuts are said to cause weakness, tremors, and fever in dogs. If you come home and the macadamia can is empty, consider a trip to the ER or induce vomiting with hydrogen peroxide.

 GRAPES AND RAISINS: Even though the specific toxin is unknown, grapes and raisins do cause kidney failure in some dogs. Snagging a couple of either may not cause harm, but if your dog eats a large quantity of grapes or raisins, you should head to the veterinary ER for a medical purge and IVs to prevent kidney problems.

YEAST DOUGH: If your dog eats a bunch of uncooked bread dough, watch for bloating or discomfort and seek veterinary assistance. Yeast dough can expand and cause gas to accumulate in your pet's stomach and intestines, causing bloating or shock.

 XYLITOL: Xylitol is used as a sweetener in many products, including gum, peanut butter, candy, baked goods, and toothpaste. Low blood sugar or elevated liver enzymes and liver failure can be seen within a few days after eating a toxic amount. A 10-pound (4.5 kg) dog could be poisoned by as little as a stick and a half of gum for hypoglycemia, whereas they would need to eat the whole pack to have liver issues. If you know your dog ate some sugarless gum with xylitol, induce vomiting as soon as possible or head to the veterinary ER.

 MILK: Some dogs may be intolerant of dairy products. Stomach and bowel upsets may also occur from eating yogurt, cottage cheese, or cheese. Milk isn't toxic, but the diarrhea that results in sensitive dogs may upset *your* stomach.

 SALT: Salty foods in large quantities may lead to lots of drinking and peeing. I would definitely avoid feeding salty chips if your dog has heart or blood pressure issues.

If you really want to share your passion for pizza with your party animal, you can find a dog-friendly recipe that has nonallergenic ingredients. (Avoid wheat flour and beef unless you know your dog can tolerate these ingredients.)

CONTROVERSIAL FOODS: FEED WITH CAUTION

These foods may cause indigestion or medical issues with your dog. Feed with caution, in moderation, or avoid them entirely.

 AVOCADO: This controversial fruit makes the list because of its irritating chemical, called *persin*. Persin may cause vomiting and diarrhea in dogs and can be fatal in birds or rodents. Avocados from South America have higher levels of persin, and some animals may be more sensitive than others. However, small amounts do not cause problems in most dogs. A veterinary friend of mine lived in an avocado orchard, and his dogs loved eating the fallen fruit. Those dogs had the most wonderful coats and even became a bit heavy. I have shared pieces of avocado with my dogs and included overripe ones in my home-cooked pet food without noticing any effects.

 ONIONS, GARLIC, CHIVES: These vegetables and herbs can cause nausea, as most plants and grass do. Onions and garlic in large quantities irritate the red blood cells. Lower doses, such as what might be found in pet foods or treats, likely will not cause a problem. I have included a small amount of garlic in my dog's food to ward off fleas and for health benefits. There doesn't seem to be a consensus on this, and some commercial dog foods and supplements contain garlic for health and flea control.

RAW OR UNDERCOOKED MEAT, EGGS, AND BONES:
Veterinarians have been taught to warn pet owners against
feeding raw meat or letting their dogs chew on raw bones. I have
encouraged my clients to feed raw, frozen, chicken wings and
breasts for years for joint nutrition and to clean their pets' teeth.
Many of my clients have fed raw meat to their dogs without
apparent harm.

FATTY MEAT: Many dogs are sensitive to a large amount of fat.
Some just get nauseous or get a case of the slimy runs. I feel that
there is a link between pancreatitis, seizures, and fatty beef. Many
sick dogs with pancreas or bowel problems, or dogs suddenly
having seizures, had a recent fatty beef meal. A lifelong dry-food
diet may only contain 10 to 20 percent fat, so a much larger
amount may send a sensitive dog's pancreas or bowels into orbit.
Use caution when feeding your dogs fatty meat or fatty poultry
skin.

BROCCOLI: Broccoli is often listed as a toxic substance, and I've
noticed that when a dog is fed a large portion of vegetables,
it can suffer from gas or diarrhea, but broccoli is not itself
particularly toxic. Fiber may loosen or firm up the stool, but
when a large quantity of veggies is added to the diet, diarrhea
may result. Dogs may suffer mild gas and diarrhea if fed a large
portion of home-cooked vegetables and meat, especially when
they are used to commercial dog food.

Sharing fatty, high-calorie human foods with your dog can lead not only to short-term stomach problems, such as vomiting and diarrhea. They can also lead to pancreatitis and debilitating obesity.

 BISCUITS, TREATS, CHEWS, AND PILL POCKETS WITH WHEAT GLUTEN: While these are not human food items that you share, I had to include them here to make sure everybody knows how much I caution owners against feeding their dogs biscuits containing wheat gluten. I think that these treats cause more problems than the rest of the list combined. Wheat treats, biscuits, and chews can cause skin and ear issues, stomach and bowel issues, anal gland issues, and seizures. If your dog has always eaten these types of treats and has no medical problems, you're lucky. Otherwise, I would avoid wheat treats and go grain free or feed healthy human food for treats.

When a dog eats something it shouldn't, you can always try to induce vomiting with 2 to 3 percent hydrogen peroxide. A small dog will take a teaspoon or two, whereas a large dog will need 2 or more tablespoons. Feeding a small meal or piece of bread before giving hydrogen peroxide may help absorb the toxin and give the poor dog something to throw up. When in doubt, always head to the veterinary ER.

KEY POINTS

1. Sharing healthy human food can enrich your dog's normal diet.

2. Lean meat, fish, eggs, healthy oils, and colorful veggies and fruits can add needed nutrients and antioxidants to the diet.

3. Slowly introducing new foods is always the key to success.

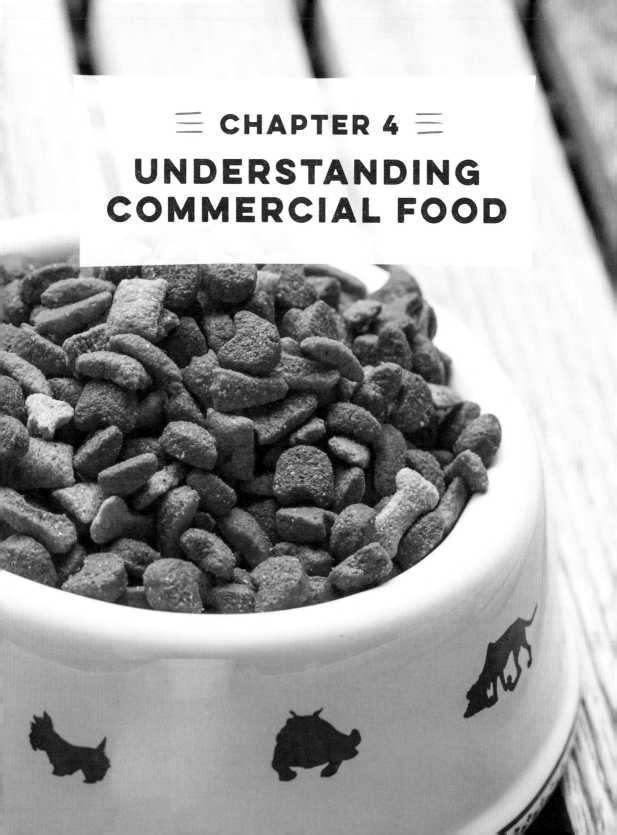

CHAPTER 4
UNDERSTANDING COMMERCIAL FOOD

PART I: DECIPHERING LABELS: PERCENTAGES, NUTRIENTS, AND INGREDIENTS

It important to know not only what ingredients go in your dog's food but also to understand the levels of essential nutrients needed in a dog's daily diet. That information comes from years of studies and feeding trials with lab animals to find the minimum levels required to prevent symptoms of deficiencies and illnesses. Feeding different amounts of critical nutrients to dogs in different life stages has revealed what levels of essential nutrients are important for normal wear and tear, pregnancy, lactation, and growth.

Doesn't it make sense that a dog that lies around most of the day needs less calcium and protein than a growing puppy, nursing mother, or sled dog? The more the demand, the more fuel is needed. For example, tremors and seizures in a nursing dog can result both from inadequate calcium in the diet and the drain from nursing pups. That lack of protein or incorrect amount of calcium can also stunt the growth and deform the bones and joints of a growing pup.

Commercial dog foods are checked against the AAFCO nutrient profile to make sure they contain the right amount of nutrients for our dogs in a couple different ways.

Computerized analysis: This method is used to determine if a recipe contains the amounts of protein, fat, minerals, and vitamins listed in the AAFCO's nutritional profile by using a database of nutritional information on each ingredient. Commercial pet food companies use this method to calculate how much chicken, tomato pomace, potato, chicken by-products, pearled barley, apple pulp, chelated minerals, vitamin A, and bone meal are needed for the nutrients to be right in a particular list of ingredients or recipe. Human recipes are often based on taste, but our dog's recipes are based on the right levels of nutrients. While computerized analysis is the easiest and cheapest way to check for the needed nutrients, it does not account for the quality of each ingredient. It assumes all animals, grains, and vegetables in the diet are the same, regardless of how they were grown, what they were fed, when they were harvested, or how they were processed.

DOCTOR'S NOTE

Scientists discovered that when animals are fed too little of a nutrient, such as a particular amino acid, essential fat, vitamin, or mineral, they may lose weight, have bone problems, get sick, develop rashes, or even die.

The nutritional profiles found on all dog foods are there to show that the product contains the right amounts of the various nutritional components your dog needs to stay active and healthy.

Foods claiming to be "breed specific" may only have a kibble size appropriate for the breed, or they may also consider the amounts of fat and calories a small, active breed, for example, is likely to burn.

Feeding trial: A feeding trial may be used to make sure the combination of nutrients from a computerized analysis of different ingredients works the way they should in a living animal. Eight dogs are fed the diet for 6 months and monitored for any signs of illness. To pass the feeding trial, six of the eight animals have to pass the tests. There are standardized feeding trial tests that use body weight, coat condition, and blood tests to evaluate the diet in question. Commercial companies may elect to run more involved feeding trials to test different diets, or they can skip the feeding trial if the diet is similar enough to another diet that has passed a feeding trial already. If the food passes the feeding trial, it is assumed to have the necessary nutrients listed in AAFCO's nutrient profile. Prescription diets that contain less nutrients than recommended by the AAFCO's nutrient profiles in order to treat medical conditions such as a lower level of protein or phosphorous in kidney failure or a lower level of magnesium to prevent bladder crystals and stones.

These methods all seem very scientific and reasonable to me, but in practice I've found that this testing doesn't always allow for a pet's individual needs. These nutritional recommendations may not address a dog's specific characteristics and biochemical variation. Some animals may need more or less nutrients in order for their body to function properly. For example, some dogs may need more moisture in the diet to prevent urinary stones, more oils for dry skin, more protein for exertion or hours of exercise, less wheat in the diet to prevent allergies (rashes and ear infections), or less fat or carbohydrates to prevent obesity and diabetes. Short feeding trials, with a limited number of breeds or dogs, can't possibly test for all the individual variations and sensitivities. So that's your job (with your vet's help). The good news here is that once you learn the differences in ingredients and how they may affect your dog, there are plenty of food choices. That's precisely the reason to learn about labels; they will help you decide which words to pay attention to.

A stroll down the pet food aisle can be overwhelming for a dog owner deciding on the right brand of food. The sheer number of choices, and the kaleidoscope of colors, shapes, and sizes of products, can make a dog owner dizzy. And, once you find what you're looking for, where is the most accurate and reliable information on the package? Is it on the front or the back?

HOW TO READ THE PACKAGE

There are only three things that are required to be displayed on the front of a pet food: the product name, the species the food is intended for, and the quantity in the bag, can, or box. Without the frills, that may look like (for example): Fish and potato, dog food, 30 pounds (13.6 kg). Boring! That wouldn't sell much food.

The display may have catchy, trendy, or popular terms in flashy type that are aimed to sell the product. Those catchy terms may appeal to you because they describe a higher-quality product or perhaps they just look really good. You may see terms such as premium, super premium, organic, grain free, free range, senior, low fat, puppy, healthy, natural, breed specific, or all life stages. Some

DOCTOR'S NOTE

Words on the front of the package may or may not mean a lot, but they are placed there to sell. The real information is in the ingredients list, so make your decision there instead of on front-label buzzwords.

terms are meaningful because they are regulated, while other terms are more evocative than nutritional. But, as I always remind my clients, not all the ingredients may be listed on the front. That is really important if you are trying to avoid ingredients that make your dog unhappy.

For example, Dr. Greg's "Premium" or "Super-Premium" Chicken and Rice Dinner sounds better than Dr. Greg's Chicken and Rice Dinner, but those words in quotations are not defined by the AAFCO or regulated in any way. They can be put on the package to sound better without proving the product *is* any better than Dr. Greg's Average Chicken and Rice Dinner. Dr. Greg's Happy, Holistic, Free-Range, Super-Premium, Chicken and Righteous Rice Dinner sounds even better, but those terms may not mean the food is any better than Dr. Greg's Regular Chicken and Rice. You get the picture. Following are some other terms you may see on the front of the bag, can, or box.

Grain free is a popular slogan, but it is not defined by the AAFCO and it may mean different things to different manufacturers. The most problematic grain for allergic dogs seems to be wheat gluten, but veterinary nutritionists are not in agreement about the role of all grains in food allergies. I argue that wheat gluten, the concentrated by-product of wheat, causes a multitude of medical issues in sensitive dogs. Other grains, such as barley and corn, may also irritate the skin, stomachs, and bowels of some dogs,

but much less commonly so than wheat gluten.

To decipher the label, you'll have to catch up on the new language of grains because some grains are taking on new names. Barley becomes pearl barley when the hull and germ layer are removed. It makes the grain sound more attractive and more nutritious than just plain barley. Wheat has a more romantic name these days as well; as consumers are increasingly avoiding wheat products, an ingredient label may proudly display "semolina" instead of "wheat." When durum wheat is milled, semolina is born. Semolina sounds prettier than wheat or wheat by-product, but semolina still contains wheat gluten.

Natural is defined by the AAFCO to mean that only natural plant, animal, or mineral sources are used. Synthetic vitamins are allowed, but nothing else from the lab for your Lab.

Organic is defined by the FDA as a food or product that has been produced or handled in compliance with the requirements of the United States Department of Agriculture's (USDA) National Organic Program. An example is grain that is not grown with synthetic pesticides or fertilizers.

Holistic suggests that the food nourishes your dog's entire system and prevents disease, but the word is not defined by any regulatory agency. It is a popular word that people associate with natural, no additives, and so on. Some brands have

Some words, such as "natural" and "organic" have specific meanings when they appear on packaging. Others, such as "holistic" and "grain-free" are buzzwords with no regulated definition.

A Jack Russell needs a kibble diet that meet his needs in terms of size and his high-energy personality.

used the term, and it fits, due to their use of human-grade ingredients and natural ingredients and preservatives.

Free range means the cow, chicken, or animal that provides the meat or eggs has access to the outside, but it is not a clearly defined term. Most meat and dairy animals live in crowded conditions.

Human grade, as defined by the AAFCO, means all ingredients are edible by humans. My home-cooked dog food is human grade.

Life stages Different life stages such as growing puppies or pregnant or nursing dogs need more calories and minerals to meet their needs. The different formulas may have more calories, different amounts of protein, calcium, phosphorus, and fat, or different size kibbles. For example, puppy formulas have more calories, more protein, balanced minerals, and smaller kibbles. Puppy mouths are smaller, so smaller kibbles are easier to eat. Adult formulas may have less fat and fewer calories for older dogs or those dogs that like to observe more than interact. There are "all life-stages" formulas that are supposed to have a balanced formula for puppies, and all adults, even pregnant or nursing. These are not magic formulas, and there is no one food that is good for every dog. You still have to monitor the weight, calories, and health of your dog. However, if you do have a puppy and adult dog that love to share each other's food, then an all life-stages diet may be the answer.

Breed-specific dog foods may just refer to the appropriate size kibble for the size of breed. It could be grain free and beef or chicken free for allergy-prone breeds. For example, breed-specific food for a Jack Russell may have smaller kibbles while food for a lab would have larger kibbles. Though these foods are designed with breeds in mind, there are no official nutritional guidelines from any organizations that are breed specific.

All breeds require the same nutrients, but individual dogs may do better on a certain meat, percentage of fat, or type of grain than others. The English bulldog, for example, has a specially shaped kibble designed for its sensitive gut issues and interesting bite. In my research, I did not see a special diet for a Puli, which is a Hungarian herding dog. That's because the breed-specific diets are designed to market to the most popular breeds at the time. It would be a rare event for a customer to ask for a "Puli diet" at the pet store. The most popular purebred dogs will get their own diets because those diets will sell more. That is a brilliant marketing strategy, but it does not mean that the purebred diet is perfect for every purebred dog.

Joint formula is not specifically defined but generally means that the diet contains ingredients with more glucosamine and chondroitin (from cartilage, windpipes, and even shrimp tails). These components have all the good stuff needed to nourish your pet's joints and keep them healthy. Arthritis occurs when the cartilage in a joint is damaged or just wears out. The idea behind feeding cartilage is by supplying all this good joint nutrition, it may support the joints and help treat or delay the onset of arthritis.

I think that it is always a good idea to nourish joints. Painful joints are common in middle-aged and older dogs. If feeding some cartilage helps prevent the onset of arthritis, or makes a dog more comfortable, then it may be helpful to include it in your canine's cuisine. You can also buy over-the-counter human glucosamine, chondroitin, MSM products, or canine glucosamine/chondroitin/MSM from your local pet store, or veterinarian. Nutrients to nourish the cartilage in the joints also come from the ends of cooked bones, raw chicken wings, and slow-cooked softened bones. My Lab loved to eat raw shrimp tails, and they are also a great source of joint nutrition.

Weight-loss and low-fat diets are formulated with lower fat to encourage weight loss or prevent pancreatitis. If the label indicates reduced calories, lite, or weight loss, then the calories need to be listed. The typical percentages of fat that make up the overall composition of the average commercial dog foods are 16 percent for dry, 23 percent for canned, and 27 percent for raw. The low-fat diets have percentages ranging from 8 to 17 percent. Low-fat prescription diets for pancreatitis are as low as 8 percent fat. Remember, these percentages do not mean the same thing as they do on labels for human food. Labeling for human food show percentages of overall daily nutrition, while dog-food labeling gives percentages of how much each nutrient contributes to the composition of the food. For example, if a food has 23 percent fat, that means 23 percent of that food is fat, it does not mean that it is giving your dog 23 percent of its daily need for fat. The protein in the better weight-loss dog foods is increased (30 to 40 percent). The carbohydrate percentage is reduced or about the same; that may be really important for some dogs that just can't lose weight on a higher carbohydrate diet. A higher-protein, lower-fat, average-carbohydrate, and a lower-calorie diet are recommended for weight loss.

You always have to measure the amount of food and monitor the dog's weight for a reduced-calorie diet to work. Keep in mind that any food can be magically turned into a weight-loss formula simply by feeding half to three-quarters the normal amount and diluting it with water. Check out the section on combating obesity for home-cooked weight-loss ideas (page 137).

Sensitive skin and **sensitive stomach** formulas are not defined. The formulas include hypoallergenic ingredients, but there is no guarantee that the "sensitive skin and stomach" formula will help solve your dog's medical issues. These formulas usually are grain free and may contain fish, rabbit, venison, kangaroo, or hydrolyzed protein as the protein portion of the diet. They will work if your dog is not allergic or intolerant to the ingredients in the formula. Every dog is an individual with its own sensitivities. I've known some dogs that could not tolerate potatoes, peas, or even tomatoes in their dog food!

HOW TO READ THE BACK AND SIDES OF THE PACKAGE

Let's move from the advertising section on the front to the labels on the sides and back of the package. The back includes the company's name and contact information, which could be helpful if you have questions or seek information about the particular food or company. Most dog food manufacturers have websites with information about their products and contact information there, as well. Beyond that, there are three required pieces of information on the labels on the back or sides of pet food containers: nutritional adequacy statements, guaranteed

EXAMPLES OF GUARANTEED ANALYSIS OF CANNED VS. DRY FOOD

NUTRIENT	CANNED	KIBBLE/DRY FOOD
Protein	10%	23%
Fat	7%	10%
Fiber	3%	5%
Water	75%	10%

DRY MATTER BASIS OF CANNED VS. DRY FOOD

NUTRIENT	CANNED	KIBBLE/DRY FOOD
Protein	40%	26%
Fat	28%	11%
Fiber	12%	5.5%
Water	n/a	n/a

These tables are similar to the guaranteed-analysis listings you find on all packages dog food. The percentages tell you how much protein, fat, fiber, and water you'll find in the container. The lower table shows what happens when the water is accounted for. That is the difference between comparing "as-fed," which is basically "as is" food served with the moisture water, or whatever juices it contain, to "dry matter basis," which means the food that still remained if the moisture was removed (imagine it being dehydrated from the "as-fed" or "as-is" diet). Once the amount of water in each type of diet is taken into account, the different nutrients can be better compared because the percentages of the nutrients are influenced by water weight.

Finding the "dry matter basis" is fairly simple. Because most dry food is 10 percent moisture, you can divide the nutrient percentage by 0.9 (or 90 percent) to get the moisture-free percentage of protein, fat, or fiber. Most canned food is 75 percent moisture, so you can divide by 0.25 (or just multiply the nutrient percentage by 4).

*Water is removed to calculate dry matter basis,

DOCTOR'S NOTE

You won't see the word "carbohydrates" on the guaranteed-analysis label, even though the carbohydrate percentage reaches 60 percent in some dry foods.

analysis, and the ingredient list. Each offers important information.

The **nutritional adequacy statements** indicate the food's intended species or life stage. For example, the Nature's Variety Instinct Raw Freeze Dried Meal or Mixer package has the nutritional adequacy statement on the back:

Complete and Balanced

Nature's Variety Instinct Raw Chicken Formula is formulated to meet the nutritional levels established by the AAFCO Dog Food Nutrient Profiles for All Life Stages

That means that this freeze-dried raw food, which my dogs love as a treat or bite to eat, has been formulated to meet the nutrient levels in the AAFCO's nutrient profiles for adults, puppies, pregnant, and nursing dogs. How do we know it has all the right stuff? The mixed ingredients have to deliver a certain level of nutrients determined by the AAFCO nutrient profiles. The nutrient levels in the freeze-

dried raw food were checked either by computer analysis and/or feeding trial.

The **guaranteed analysis** presents itself as a list, chart, or paragraph, and appears on the side or back of the package of dog food. The major purpose of the guaranteed analysis is to allow you to compare major nutrients and calories between foods. These can vary quite a bit. You may decide that your working dog needs more protein or fat or that your weight-challenged dog needs fewer carbohydrates, more fiber, or less fat. You'll use the numbers in the guaranteed analysis to compare the protein and fat levels in different dry, canned, dehydrated, or raw foods. That sounds easy enough, doesn't it? Not so fast. You also need to take into account the amount of moisture in the container (can, bag, or pouch)—and mentally remove it—to accurately compare the nutrients in canned and dry food.

DRY MATTER: HOW TO COMPARE THE NUTRIENTS IN DIFFERENT TYPES OF DOG FOOD

When deciding between a canned or dry food (or semimoist or raw), you'll need to mentally remove the moisture from the "as-fed" diet using the calculation given in the guaranteed analysis chart or in the shortcut below to best identify the proper food for your dog. For example, let's say you want less fat in your dog's diet, due to his chronic pancreatitis. Without this formula, you may think the canned food in the chart on page 79 has less fat (the label shows 7% fat in the guaranteed analysis). However, when accounting for the amount of moisture in the canned food (75% water), the true fat percentage is four times the amount shown in the guaranteed analysis (28%)! Dry food, in fact, has a lower percentage (11%) of fat than the canned food.

So while a nutrient such as protein initially looks much lower in the canned food than it does in the kibble, that is only because it is diluted by the water in the canned food. Only after you mentally extract the water in the moister foods can the percentages of nutrients be more accurately compared.

Here's the shortcut for most canned and raw foods: If the canned or raw food contains around 75 percent moisture (see "water" in the table), multiply the percentage of each nutrient by four. Try multiplying the different nutrients in the guaranteed analysis under the canned food as-fed by four and you'll get the dry matter basis chart percentages under canned food, making you a math wizard. This really is the only way you can compare the percentages of protein or fat in moister, canned or raw food with the drier kibble or freeze-dried food.

FINDING CARBOHYDRATES ON THE LABEL

You won't see the word "carbohydrates" on the guaranteed analysis label, even though the carbohydrate percentage reaches 60 percent in some dry foods. Why is that? I'm not really sure, because it is certainly prominently displayed on the analysis labels of human food. Is a high level of carbohydrates a problem for dogs? The answer to that is uncertain and constantly debated. Carbohydrates are not essential to our domesticated carnivores, and that particular nutrient may not be the best fuel for them. I think it is a good idea to keep the amount of this controversial nutrient closer to the ancestral levels (14 percent) than the high level in some dry food (60 percent). I try to feed diets with the carbohydrates in the 30 to 40 percent range. Note, that percentage includes the percentage of fiber, which is a carbohydrate.

Feeding your dog high-quality foods can help control weight and cope with a range of medical issues.

DOCTOR'S NOTE

Any time the words "formula," "dinner," "blend," or "mix" appear as a descriptive term, the diet can also have other meats, poultry, or fish mixed in as well as the meat listed in the name. So a "salmon dinner" might actually contain salmon and chicken, which is important to know if you dog is allergic or sensitive to chicken.

To find the amount of carbohydrates in your dog's food, you can follow the following steps. Let's use the percentages from canned food we already used as an example to find the "hidden" carbohydrate, using the guaranteed analysis chart on page 79.

1. Add the percentages of protein, fat, and water (do not include fiber, which is a carbohydrate) from the guaranteed analysis.

10 + 7 + 75 = 92%

2. Subtract that percentage from 100 to get the amount of carbohydrates.

100 – 92 = 8%

3. Use the following formula to find the dry matter basis. Percent of the nutrient / (100% water)

8 / 25 = 0.32, or 32%

This canned food has about 32% carbohydrates, safely in the 30- to 40-percent range I recommend. You can repeat these steps to find the amount of carbohydrates in dry food or other types of food.

Most dry foods contain a higher percentage of carbohydrates, whereas canned and other moist foods have a lower amount. This may be very important if you want to feed your dog a lower level of carbs to be closer to the ancestral level, to address a medical problem such as diabetes, or for a dog that just doesn't lose weight on a low-fat diet. Future research may shed light on the role this nutrient plays in our dogs. For now, I'm inclined to feed more protein and fat and less carbs than you'll find in most commercial dry food.

OTHER INGREDIENTS ON THE GUARANTEED ANALYSIS

Dietary fiber is the edible part of plants—the leaves, seeds, stems, fruit, vegetables, and grains—that resists digestion. It is chewed and softened but not broken down and absorbed. There are two types of fiber that can help your dog.

Insoluble fiber is composed of indigestible fibers that accomplish several things in the bowels. First, the bulk of the insoluble fiber gives the intestines something to push against and helps matter progress toward the rear. This action may speed up the bowel and have a laxative effect. The insoluble fiber in bulkier stool may also help massage those anal glands that are reluctant to empty due to poor plumbing. Sources of insoluble fiber are whole grains, barley, brown rice, zucchini, celery, broccoli, tomatoes, carrots, green beans, dark leafy vegetables, and fruit.

THE ELIMINATION DIET

When we think a dog has a food issue, the elimination diet, also called a food trial, is the gold standard for deciding what ingredients (if any) are causing the issues. To perform this diet, a single meat, poultry, or fish protein and its corresponding fat and a single carbohydrate are combined into a hypoallergenic diet and given to the dog for two months to see if the issues clear up. Duck/potato, fish/potato, venison/potato, rabbit/potato, and kangaroo/oats are common examples of diets used when dogs have moderate-to-severe skin, ear, or bowel issues. Potato is a common bland carbohydrate, but some dogs are even intolerant or allergic to potatoes! Sweet potato, peas, lentils, tapioca, brown rice, and garbanzo beans are other novel carbohydrates you will see in limited ingredient diets. If a dog is successful on a limited-ingredient diet, other foods can be introduced one at a time to see if they can be tolerated. For more on this, see Food Trials for Allergens on page 150.

DOCTOR'S NOTE

Common vegetable sources of fiber that are good for your dog are pumpkin, canned green beans, peas and carrots, apples, or mini carrots. Common non-gluten grains used to increase fiber are oatmeal and barley. Introduce vegetables and fruit as 10 to 20 percent of your dog's diet for extra phytonutrients, prebiotics, and fiber.

Soluble fiber isn't digestible but gets gelatinous in water and can be fermented by the bacteria in the colon. This type of fiber can absorb water and may help slow down the bowel. This can give your chubby pet a feeling of fullness and help him lose weight. The fiber in the bowel may also slow the absorption of sugars and help control blood sugar. A slower bowel allows the return of water to the body. This may help with diarrhea. Examples of soluble fibers for dogs are oatmeal, lentils, apples, flaxseeds, beans, peas, psyllium, celery, and carrots. Soluble fiber is also a prebiotic. The dissolved indigestible carbohydrates feed the friendly bacteria in the colon. They, in turn, crank out volatile fatty acids that nourish the cells of the colon. These helpful bacteria line the surface of the intestine and colon, forming a bacterial barrier to help keep the bacteria such as salmonella and *E. coli* out. The prebiotics, or soluble fiber, nourish your dog's bacterial friends, which, in turn, nourish and protect them. These bacteria and the chemicals they produce may help decrease inflammation in many places in a dog's body. That's why prebiotics are so important.

Most dry dog foods contain 3 to 5 percent fiber, but some prescription weight-loss or diabetes formulas may include up to 30 percent fiber. More fiber can dilute the calories in any diet and help dogs lose weight or slow down the absorption of carbohydrates to help a diabetic dog regulate his blood sugar. Extra fiber may also help put "the squeeze" on anal glands that don't empty correctly.

So how can you add fiber to your dog's diet outside those prescription foods?

Adding one teaspoon to one tablespoon of Metamucil or a portion of vegetables (10 to 20 percent of your dog's daily intake) to the food daily (or several times a week) will add bulk, soften the stool, and reduce calories.

Although ash is not listed in the guaranteed analysis (see page 79), you may see it included with the moisture, protein, fat, or fiber on the package of other commercial foods. Ash is left after a food is completely incinerated during processing. The percentage of ash is the percentage of minerals in the food. If food is incinerated in a nutritional oven called a *bomb calorimeter*, only the minerals remain. They can be weighed and expressed as a percentage of the food.

DOCTOR'S NOTE

The most popular dog food is dry food, or kibble, which requires our dogs to drink more water for digestion and to make up for the lack of moisture in the food.

UNDERSTANDING THE INGREDIENTS LIST

The ingredients list is by far the most important tool that you can use to evaluate dog food. It is in this list that you will see the type of meat used; the type of fat added; the type of carbohydrate used; and the vitamins, minerals, antioxidants, and preservatives mixed in.

The label will always have the ingredients listed in the order of the proportions they are present in the food. For example:

Rabbit, chicken meal, menhaden fish meal (source of omega-3 fatty acids, DHA, and EPA), chicken fat (preserved with mixed tocopherols), deboned chicken, dried egg

This ingredients list is from a popular brand and is called a "rabbit formula." The rabbit meat needs to be only 25 percent of the weight of the mix to use "rabbit" as the primary name. This is called the 25 percent, or dinner labeling, rule.

By law, an ingredient that is present in the highest concentration in the diet has to

DOCTOR'S NOTE

Moister foods (canned or home cooked) usually have fewer calories per ounce, contain more water to aid kidney function, and may decrease the incidence of urinary crystals and bladder stones.

be listed first, and the percentage of the ingredient decreases as it appears farther down on the label. However, ingredients can also be processed and broken down and, as a result, can be positioned lower on the ingredient list. For example, corn should be listed first in a commercial food that contains more corn than chicken, but if the corn is split into two processed parts, cornmeal and corn gluten, then they can be listed after more appealing ingredients such as chicken.

Before we split the corn into its processed ingredients, a potential ingredient list could read: corn, chicken, but after we split it, the ingredient list would look like this: chicken, corn meal, corn gluten. Which would you be inclined to buy? "Neither" is probably the right answer, but having the chicken appear first makes the diet sound better.

Ingredient labels don't always tell the truth about the animals contained in the food, and there is a chance that some unlisted protein ingredients are in the food. A study a few years back by D.M. Raditic, R.L. Remillard, and K.C. Tater tested the claims of some commercial, limited-ingredient, venison diets. The findings showed that proteins such as soy and beef were present in the foods they tested, even though those ingredients were not listed anywhere on the packaging.

BY-PRODUCTS

So what are by-products, anyway? Animal by-products are the nonrendered, cleaned parts of slaughtered animals, including the viscera (internal organs of chest and abdomen), head, and feet, that are free from fecal content and foreign material. If you steam or heat treat the by-products and take out the fat, the ground-up, rendered protein is called meal.

Poultry meal is defined as the dry, rendered product from a combination of clean flesh and skin with or without accompanying bone, derived from the parts of whole carcasses of poultry or a combination thereof, exclusive of feathers, heads, feet, and entrails. Check the AAFCO website for more definitions and information: www.aafco.org/Consumers/What-is-in-Pet-Food.

Let's consider the diet of our dog's ancestors. They ate prey, which included muscle, joints, liver, heart, trachea, lungs, intestines, skin, bones, feathers, scales, and hair. It is certain that our dog's ancestors enjoyed by-products, but the percentage of muscle or meat was probably higher than in some commercial dog foods that rely on meat and meal by-products to supply all the protein in the recipe. That's why I'm a fan of real muscle in dog food. Some pets may need more protein than the 18 to 22 percent required in commercial foods, and I haven't been able to find a definitive answer to know if heat-treated and processed by-products or meal still supply the quality of protein that our dogs need.

Our pets' ancestors ate a good deal of muscles and organs, and my personal feeling is that our dogs need more than the minimum processed amount. I always make sure my dogs' diets—whether canned, raw, dehydrated, freeze-dried, or shared human food—have some real muscle and organs in the mix.

If you are trying to eliminate ingredients from your dog's diet to pin down the source of ailments such as skin problems or lethargy, avoid foods labeled as "blends" as they may contain surprising, and perhaps even hidden, ingredients.

Remember, just because the label says it contains a certain animal, bird, or fish, or is supposed to be grain free, there is no guarantee, and the label on the front or the back may not be accurate. Unlisted ingredients become especially important if your pet is unable to tolerate wheat gluten, beef, chicken, or other ingredients in the diet. Similarly, limited-ingredient diets do not always contain all the ingredients listed on the label. This becomes especially important in an elimination diet, used to find out which ingredients work best for your dog. Prescription limited-ingredient diets such as kangaroo and oats, or a prescription-hydrolyzed diet, are more lilely to contain the best choices if this is what you're doing.

If the wording of a limited-ingredient diet says "rabbit and potato," that is probably what is inside. If the label says "rabbit and potato" *and* "blend," "formula," "with," "dinner," "plate," or other modifiers, then the food may contain other parts of different animals. Of course, you also need to check the label for added "meat, by-products, or fats" where no animal is listed. In an elimination diet, you want to use only one animal, such as rabbit by-products, rabbit fat, or rabbit meal, instead of just "animal fat, by-products, digest, or meal." Kangaroo and oats is a veterinary formula that, according to the study I referred to, may be more reliable about containing the ingredients appearing on the label.

WATER

Water has a very important place in our dog's diet, though it is not listed in the required nutrient profiles or in the list of ingredients. It is, however, listed in the guaranteed analysis as the percentage of moisture in the diet: 10 percent for dry foods, 30 to 75 percent for moist and raw foods, and 75 to 80 percent for moist or "soupy" canned foods. For those dogs that don't drink enough from a bowl, it can be a very important ingredient in food. On the other hand, some dogs make up for the dryness of their food by drinking too much water and then having to pee all the time. Feeding them a canned or moister diet seems to avoid this issue. While tap or filtered water is the most economical, you can also add canned food and chicken broth to make dry food moister and taste better.

If your dog does not have medical issues and stays at the right weight, then a diet of dry food may work just fine. But dogs with medical issues may need more water in their diet. Those with sensitive stomachs seem to handle moister food a bit better. Dogs that have the tendency to form bladder stones and crystals may not form them with a moister diet. Obese dogs may lose weight when moister canned food is fed instead of dry food.

PROTEIN AND FAT

The most common ingredients to meet your pet's protein and fat requirements include meat, fish, animal carcasses, organs, dairy products, eggs, and soy. The quality and cost of the food is largely determined by the parts of the animal used. When I cook for my dogs, I know what protein and fat goes in their bowl. When I feed canned food, raw food, or dehydrated food, I depend on the label to give me information on the types and parts of the animals that were used in the recipe. I also feed a variety of foods and diets—something I strongly urge pet owners to do. Following are examples of various types of foods I feed my dogs and an economical dry food for comparison. The different foods I use supply a healthful variety of ingredients.

DOCTOR'S NOTE

Carbohydrates aren't all bad. Whole gluten-free grains and rice can be a good source of fiber and contain important nutrients. Colorful veggies and sweet potatoes contain important vitamins, fiber, and antioxidants.

HOME-COOKED FOODS

Ingredients: skinless, boneless chicken breasts; chicken wings; chicken livers; chicken hearts and gizzards; eggs.

CANNED FOODS

Chicken-stew ingredients: chicken and chicken liver, muscle, and carcass with more liver added; the skin of the chicken skin contains the fat.

Duck-and-potato ingredients: duck, duck liver, and duck by-product meal. (This duck and potato canned food has by-products instead of just duck. The rest of the meat, organ, and fats are listed by animal.)

DEHYDRATED FOODS

Ingredients: turkey and organic flax, with "cage-free" turkey on the front of the package. The flaxseed is added to boost the omega fatty acids. The flaxseed is organic and free of pesticides and other chemicals. Protein and fat is from the turkey, and some healthy oils come from the flaxseed.

RAW FOODS

Chicken-formula ingredients: chicken (including raw chicken bone), turkey, turkey liver, and turkey heart. The words "chicken formula" appear on the package.

Rabbit-formula ingredients: rabbit (including ground rabbit bone), pork liver, pork heart, pork fat, ground pork bone, and rabbit liver.

Freeze-dried ingredients: chicken (ground with bone), chicken liver, chicken gizzard.

DRY DOG FOODS

There are many excellent dry-food brands that contain great ingredients. I like my dogs to eat moister food, but dry food is more economical and easier to feed. Consider moister food with dogs that have skin, ear, gut, kidney or urinary problems.

For comparison, the following ingredients are taken from the label of an economical dog food. Dry dog-food ingredients: chicken by-product meal, animal fat preserved with mixed tocopherols, beef, meat, and bone meal.

In this example, the chicken is a by-product meal and that translates to less muscle and more of the stripped carcass and organs. The term "animal fat" may mean a mix of fats from different animals, including chicken, turkey, beef, and pork. Bovine muscle is included and is listed as beef. Meat and bone meal means muscle and bone from some carcasses or meaty bones were ground up and included. You may not even want to know where they came from but probably wouldn't use them if you did. I would avoid by-products and meals that don't specify an animal source. A limited-ingredient diet for sensitive or allergic dogs should

If you're feeding your dog home-cooked food, variety can keep them happy and healthy. If they're sensitive or allergic, you may do better sticking to a diet that has one source of meat, fat, and carbohydrates.

contain only one meat/fat and one source of carbohydrates. There's really no way to tell how much beef or meat meal is in the recipe. The position of chicken by-product meal on the ingredients list suggests that there is more of that and animal fat than beef and meat meal.

CARBOHYDRATES

Now let's look at the carbohydrate ingredients in the foods I feed my dogs and in an example of a Hill's Science Diet dry food.

CARBOHYDRATES IN HOME-COOKED FOODS

Green beans, peas, carrots, broccoli, sweet potatoes, garbanzo beans, and brown rice

CARBOHYDRATES IN CANNED FOODS: CHICKEN AND RICE

Brown rice, whole carrots, sweet potatoes, peas, blueberries, and cranberries.

Brown rice has more nutrients than white rice, and the mix of colorful vegetables and fruit combine to provide many nutrients. Rice is considered a grain but is gluten free.

CARBOHYDRATES IN DEHYDRATED FOODS

Organic oats, potatoes, carrots, cabbage, organic kelp, apples, and honey.

This is another good mix of veggies and fruit. Kelp is a natural source of many minerals. Oats are a good source of fiber and are gluten free. A variety of vegetables provides the greatest mix of nutrients and decreases the need for synthetic ones. For allergic dogs, oats, rice, potatoes, peas, or lentils are common carbohydrate sources.

CARBOHYDRATES IN HILL'S SCIENCE DIET

Brown rice, whole grain oats, whole grain barley, yellow peas, dried beet pulp, vegetable and fruit blend (green peas, apples, cranberries, carrots, and broccoli).

This ingredient list has whole grains, gluten grains, and a vegetable-and-fruit blend.

Dogs that can't handle whole grains may be in the minority, but if your dog reacts adversely to grains in food, then it may be barley intolerant. If this is the case, there are other ways to supply carbohydrates and fiber. Even though vegetables and fruits appear on the label, the farther down the list they are, they become a less important source of carbs.

CARBOHYDRATES IN ECONOMICAL FOODS

Grains are not the only carbohydrates that are used in commercial dog food. With popular support of wheat products on the decline, you'll see more nongluten grains, such as rice and oats, along with other carbohydrates, such as potatoes, carrots, corn, peas, beets, green beans, and squash, in the list of ingredients.

Economical commercial dog foods may feature vegetables prominently on their packaging, but the pictures don't necessarily match what is inside. You'll see beautiful wheat plants and a colorful ear of corn along with whole carrots and parsley. The picture brings a flavorful stew to mind . . . until you examine the carbohydrate ingredients of the "Healthy Radiance" mix: ground yellow cornmeal, corn gluten meal, whole wheat flour, rice flour, soy flour, sugar, dried sweet potatoes, dried green beans, and dried carrots.

Not all carbohydrates are created equal. Look for foods that contain veggies, such as sweet potatoes and carrots, over corn and flour.

DOCTOR'S NOTE

Remember, the cheaper grain by-products make the dog food more economical and profitable for manufacturers, but it is a low-quality fuel for your furry friends.

The ingredient label from this package lists carbohydrates, such as corn and corn gluten, followed by wheat flour. The three dried veggies from the picture on the front are the last carbs on the list. Labeling recommendations from AAFCO dictate that the ingredients with the largest amounts come first, but even sugar and salt are listed *before* the veggies. This means there may only be a sprinkling of dried sweet potato, green beans, carrots, and parsley powder in the recipe.

What kind of carbohydrates should you look for on the label? Here are the ones found in Merrick's canned food: sweet potatoes, peas, potatoes, apples, blueberries, organic alfalfa. Merrick advertises fresh, whole ingredients, and their ingredient label backs up that claim. These kinds of carbohydrates bring additional vitamins to the bowl instead of nutrient-poor processed carbohydrates such as grain by-products.

VITAMINS, MINERALS, ANTIOXIDANTS, THICKENING AGENTS, AND PRESERVATIVES

Food labels often include long lists of ingredients that are difficult to understand. This section is intended to help you understand what these ingredients truly mean, as well as their benefits or harmful effects.

A FEW WORDS ABOUT PRESERVATIVES

Commercial dog food, and especially dry food, needs to be preserved in order to remain safe and edible. This means pet foods may contain preservatives as well as synthetic or natural antioxidants; these additives ensure that the fat does not become rancid and mold will not grow. Some synthetic antioxidants and preservatives, such as BHA, BHT, TBHQ, are suspected of causing cancer, and ethoxyquin may be linked to liver and skin problems. The FDA considers them safe at the levels used in food, but who really knows the truth in today's complicated maze of food processing? I would rather have natural antioxidants and preservatives, such as ascorbate or tocopherols, known as vitamin C or vitamin E, preserving my dogs' food. Why use a questionable ingredient?

Once you get used to reading ingredients, it becomes easier to compare different brands and see how different they can be.

Let's compare two different sample diets to see which one you would pick for your loved, furry family member.

DIET 1: Rabbit (including ground rabbit bone), pork liver, pork heart, pork fat, ground pork bone, rabbit liver, yeast culture, pumpkinseeds, montmorillonite clay, apples, broccoli, butternut squash, rabbit kidney, rabbit lung, salt, cod liver oil, dried kelp, carrots, spinach, dried chicory root, blueberries (continued on p. 100)

SAMPLE DRY FOOD INGREDIENT LIST

Below are condensed labels from several types of dog food. Notice that the list becomes shorter when more meat, organ meat, fruit, and veggies are used in the recipe, while more economical foods need synthetic vitamins, minerals, antioxidants, and preservatives added.

We'll start by looking at the more economical foods with the longest lists of ingredients. Cheaper foods filled with by-products and processed grain ingredients may contain fewer natural nutrients, so more synthetic nutrients are needed and the ingredient list is quite large. You'll notice as we look at better quality foods, the size of the list will shrink. More economical commercial dry foods contain a list of ingredients like this:

Animal fat preserved with mixed tocopherols: a form of vitamin E, but not a good vitamin E supplement, it is used as an antioxidant or preservative so fat doesn't go rancid.

Propylene glycol: keeps food from drying out; it is also used in cosmetics but is banned in cat food.

Tricalcium phosphate: a source of calcium and phosphorus; it is important for bone structure and muscle function.

Phosphoric acid: used for flavoring; it is an emulsifier and inhibits discoloration.

Potassium chloride: a source of potassium; it is important for muscle and nerve function.

Sorbic acid: a natural, organic preservative to prohibit growth of molds, yeast, and fungi.

Calcium propionate: a preservative and mold inhibitor commonly used in bakery products.

Choline chloride: an essential nutrient important for nerve function and growth.

l-lysine monohydrochloride: an essential amino acid present in meat.

Zinc sulfate: a source of trace mineral zinc important for the health of skin and digestion.

Red 40, yellow 6, yellow 5, and blue 2: synthetic dyes (food coloring) for human visual appeal only. These dyes may be responsible for some chronic medical problems such as chronic skin and bowel issues.

Ferrous sulfate: a source of iron; the iron molecule is a part of hemoglobin in red blood cells that transports oxygen.

Manganese sulfate: a source of manganese, important in enzymes and nerve function; it is also an antioxidant.

Calcium carbonate: a source of calcium.

Copper sulfate: a source of copper, needed to absorb iron and prevent anemia.

Brewers dried yeast: a source of B vitamins and saccharomyces probiotic.

Calcium pantothenate: a source of vitamin B–like pantothenic acid.

Garlic oil: a natural antioxidant often used as a flea repellent.

Menadione sodium bisulfite complex: a synthetic source of vitamin K activity. Reported side effects make it a questionable additive. Vitamin K is made naturally by your dog's intestinal microbes or gut flora.

Calcium iodate: a source of iodine.

Folic acid: necessary for the production and maintenance of new cells and in DNA and RNA synthesis.

Sodium selenite: a source of selenium, which protects against oxidants.

Foods may also contain vitamins A (for vision and healthy skin), B_1 (from thiamine mononitrate), B_2 (from riboflavin, for energy metabolism and healthy skin), B_3 (from niacin, for energy metabolism of every single cell), B_6 (from pyridoxine hydrochloride, for amino acid and fatty acid metabolism and converting tryptophan to niacin and to serotonin), B_7 (from biotin, for energy metabolism and the synthesis of fat and glycogen), B_{12} (for digestion and nerve function), D_3 (for calcium regulation), E (a natural antioxidant and muscle nutrient), and salt.

A commercial food with a long, complicated label contains many synthetic vitamin and mineral additives. If it contained more muscle, liver, and other nutritious ingredients, instead of by-products, fewer synthetic ingredients would need to be added.

HEALTHIER BRANDS OF DRY DOG FOOD MAY LIST ADDITIONAL INGREDIENTS AS FOLLOWS:

Copper amino acid chelate: organic forms of essential trace minerals, such as copper, iron, manganese, and zinc. Animals absorb, digest, and use mineral chelates better than inorganic minerals, which means that lower concentrations can be used.

Caramel: natural food coloring, but still only for human visual appeal.

Dried yeast: a source of saccharomyces cerevisiae. Probiotics like saccharomyces and other fermentation products (dried lactobacillus acidophilus and dried bacillus subtilis) help the bowel maintain a healthy colony of yeast and bacteria. Probiotics can help prevent infection by bacteria such as *E.coli* or salmonella and protozoa such as giardia. These fermentation products are active dehydrated cultures that become active when hydrated and warmed in the gut. They may aid in digestion, improve colon and rectum health, and prevent diarrhea.

Other ingredients may include iron amino acid chelate, zinc amino acid chelate, manganese amino acid chelate, choline chloride, sodium selenite, salt, potassium chloride, calcium carbonate, and dicalcium phosphate. You may also see vitamins A, B (from thiamine mononitrate), B_2 (from riboflavin), B_3 (from niacin), B_5 (from d-calcium pantothenate), B_6 (from pyridoxine hydrochloride), B_7 (from biotin), B_9 (from folic acid), B_{12}, C (from calcium ascorbate), D_3, and E.

SAMPLE CANNED FOOD INGREDIENT LIST

The canned commercial dog foods that I feed my dogs are grain free and contain fewer synthetic vitamins, minerals, antioxidants, and preservatives because they contain better ingredients and need fewer preservatives.

Guar gum: a thickener and stabilizer in canned food, it is made up of ground guar beans; it is a highly soluble and highly digestible prebiotic fiber that promotes intestinal health.

Ground flaxseed: a source of omega-3 and omega-6 fatty acids, less potent than omega-3 from fish and krill oil.

Carrageenan: a natural red kelp ingredient used as a thickener and stabilizer in canned food. Avoid it if your dog has a sensitive gut.

Fish oil: a natural source of omega-3 and omega-6 from fish. Nutritional data suggests that omega-3 fatty acids are beneficial for the function of many different organs. Your dog may also benefit from additional omega-3 supplements.

Other ingredients may include potassium chloride, salt, iron amino acid chelate, zinc amino acid chelate, cobalt amino acid chelate, manganese amino acid chelate, sodium selenite, potassium iodide, and choline chloride. Canned food also may contain vitamins A, B (from thiamine mononitrate), B_2 (from riboflavin), B_7 (from biotin), B_{12}, D_3, and E.

DEHYDRATED FOOD INGREDIENTS

Dehydrated, "natural" food may have even fewer remaining ingredients, because the vitamins and trace minerals are present in a variety of natural food ingredients in the diet. You won't see synthetic preservatives or other additives. These diets are more expensive.

In addition to the whole ingredients in dehydrated foods, possible ingredients include tricalcium phosphate, choline chloride, zinc amino acid chelate, potassium iodide, potassium chloride, iron amino acid chelate, copper amino acid chelate, as well as vitamins D_3 and E.

RAW-FOOD DIET INGREDIENTS

The ingredients list for a raw-food diet is likely the shortest you can find. While I don't think everyone needs to feed raw food, it doesn't hurt to make some raw food part of your dog's menu. The right combination of meat, organs, bone, salt, cod oil, and a variety of vegetables can go a long way in supplying needed nutrients. The list of vitamins, minerals, and preservatives usually present in economical foods isn't present in the raw food I feed my dogs. In fact, the only natural ingredient added is montmorillonite clay, which isn't a vitamin, mineral, or preservative, but absorbs contaminants or heavy metals (such as mercury or toxins) and flushes them out of the body through the dog's colon.

The list of additives and ingredients shrinks from more than thirty in the economical dry food to many fewer in the canned and dehydrated food, to one in the raw food. Partly it's because all essential vitamins are present in less-processed foods and, therefore, do not have to be added ingredients, though calcium and some trace minerals are still added. In nutritional matters, it is important to consider nature and science. For optimum nutrition, some supplemental ingredients may be needed. The more natural ingredients used, the more natural combinations of healthful ingredients and the less vitamins and minerals that will need to be added.

Note: Some explanations of the ingredients were derived from the Blue Buffalo Additive Glossary. Check it out at bluebuffalo.com/ingredients.

DIET 2: Whole grain corn, meat and bone meal, corn gluten meal, animal fat preserved with mixed tocopherols, soybean meal, poultry by-product meal, egg and chicken flavor, whole grain wheat, animal digest, salt, calcium carbonate, potassium chloride, dicalcium phosphate, choline chloride, zinc sulfate, yellow 6, vitamin E supplement, l-lysine monohydrochloride, ferrous sulfate, yellow 5, red 40, manganese sulfate, niacin, blue 2, vitamin a supplement, copper sulfate, calcium pantothenate, garlic oil, pyridoxine hydrochloride, vitamin B_{12} supplement, thiamine mononitrate, vitamin D_3 supplement, riboflavin supplement, calcium iodate, menadione sodium bisulfite complex, folic acid, biotin, sodium selenite, B-4101

Read the ingredients list closely. Which is the more economical one? Which one would be better for your dog? I used to think that a long ingredient list filled with familiar names of vitamins and minerals meant that the diet was fortified. The reverse is actually more accurate. So which is the better choice?

DIET 1: has named sources of meat and fat, as well as a healthy mix of colorful vegetables and blueberries. It does not contain any stabilizers, thickeners, preservatives, or synthetic chemicals. This diet would be a much more healthful one. Higher-quality dry, canned, raw, dehydrated, or home-cooked food will contain better ingredients and need fewer additives.

DIET 2: has whole grain corn gluten and wheat as the carbohydrate (corn gluten may be used to increase the protein, but it is an incomplete protein lacking essential amino acids, which often causes medical issues). Meat meal, animal digest, poultry by-product meal, soybean meal, and animal fat are the sources of protein and fat and suggest a highly processed mix of unknown animals. There is absolutely no reason to have synthetic dyes for animals that live in the limited spectrum of brown, yellow, gray, and blue. The colors are for us! The list of vitamins and minerals round out the diet to make up for the lack of organs, vegetables, and fruit. Menadione sodium bisulfate is a form of synthetic vitamin K. This synthetic vitamin is controversial and unneeded because the bacteria and a healthy colon supply natural vitamin K.

To check out dog food rated on the basis of ingredients, processing, and recall history, see Dog Food Advisor (dogfoodadvisor.com). They have rated thousands of foods and make the work of evaluating dog food easier for you.

Nature has provided nourishment to all that lived on this planet for eons. Nutritionists and chemists are learning her secrets, but we may not know them all yet. Nature may know about obscure interactions between molecules and minerals that help organs or muscles work better or help the immune system fight infection or cancer.

Feeding your dog high-quality foods can help control weight and cope with a range of medical issues.

In practice, I've learned that individual dogs may need different ingredients to cope with weight or other medical issues. The ingredients in a commercial mix may be "complete and balanced" for the average dog but not for the obese Lab or terribly allergic bulldog. The food that you decide to feed your dog will depend on the value that you see in better quality ingredients. I advise you to feed the best ingredients you can afford, but in general, I advise feeding medium-to-higher priced food from well-known brands with the particular animal ingredients listed instead of meal or by-products that do not list a specific animal source.

PART II: THE RELATIONSHIP BETWEEN INGREDIENTS AND NUTRIENTS

Now that you better understand how to read the ingredients on food labels, this part of the chapter will help you make the most of that information and determine how much of those nutrients and ingredients your dog needs. As we've learned, nutrients are the building blocks of all the ingredients (animals, plants, and synthetic chemicals) that keep your dog's machine running. The ingredients in commercial foods are blended in proportions designed to ensure the required nutrients are at the correct level in the final diet and meet the AAFCO's nutrient profile guidelines. Ingredients have names such as chicken, beef, liver, egg, salmon, alfalfa, barley, potato, bone meal, calcium triphosphate, carrots, tocopherols, and menadione, and they contain essential nutrients such as protein, fat, carbohydrate, fiber, minerals, and vitamins. If a certain mix of primary ingredients (corn gluten, corn meal, chicken by-products, bone meal, animal fat, wheat by-products) lacks the necessary vitamins or minerals (as a list of by-products like this would) those vitamins or minerals are added and listed as ingredients to make up the final profile of needed nutrients.

The recipes or mix of ingredients in any one dog food needs to contain protein, fat, vitamins, and minerals in the right amounts and proportions. For example, calcium has to be at least equal to, but not more than, twice the amount of phosphorus (1:1 to 2:1 ratio) so that the body can easily store or retrieve them from the bones without causing structural problems. Just as poor building materials result in a building collapse, if the body doesn't have what it needs in the right proportions, it will weaken. In the case of the bones, faulty construction or repair can lead to medical problems, such as arthritis. If the ingredients in the recipe don't contain the right amino acids or the right kind of fats, then the body may substitute inferior combinations that won't work as well.

MOISTURE CONTENT

Every dog should have access to plenty of fresh water. And, believe it or not, moisture is a nutrient listed on the guaranteed analysis (see page 136 for more on guaranteed analysis). All commercial pet food contains a certain amount of moisture, depending on the type of food. Dry, dehydrated, and freeze-dried foods contain the least (10 percent) while canned, home-cooked, or raw may contain the most (40 to 80 percent).

Enough moisture decreases the amount of digestive juices needed and helps the kidneys filter out waste products. Increased moisture in the diet may help prevent the formation of urinary crystals and stones as it dilutes the urine. If you cut the normal ration of dry food to one-half to two-thirds and add moisture, such as water or low-fat broth, this reduces the calories and makes the weight-challenged dogs feel just as full with less!

PROTEIN AND FAT RATIOS

Imagine your vet said that your slightly chunky older dog needs 20 percent protein and 10 percent fat for his kidney problems, pancreatitis, and weight loss. You know your dog likes canned food better, and you would like to be able to feed that. You've settled on a well-known brand with excellent ingredients and now you're looking for their specific food that has the percentage of nutrients that your vet recommended. Senior diets can contain less fat and protein and can be good choices for dogs that are prone to these types of health problems. What percentages of protein and fat would you look for in a moister food? Remember the shortcut we learned earlier: If a can of food is around 75% water, multiply the nutrient percentage by 4 to find out the nutrients in the dry matter basis of food. Let's reverse that to go from the percentage your vet advised in the dry food to the amount to look for in canned

food. If you divided the 20 percent protein and 10 percent fat by four, then you'll get the approximate numbers to look for. The senior diet canned food should contain approximately 5 percent protein and 2.5 percent fat.

Protein levels can vary widely in commercial foods. You will rarely see AAFCO's minimum protein requirement of 18 to 22 percent protein on a package. Instead, most commercial dog foods are above that, with levels from 20 to 30 percent protein, and high-protein foods, such as raw food, can range from 35 to 50 percent protein. Low-protein senior diets and renal or kidney diets can run from 11 to 20 percent protein. Protein restriction is important when the kidneys are failing and the liver is really impaired, but some experts argue that a diet with a poor protein or too low in protein isn't a good idea when the kidneys or liver have only mild medical issues. The kidneys, liver, heart, and muscle need quality protein to work right, and protein starving may help one organ that is struggling while making other organs or muscles work harder. When the kidneys are failing, limiting phosphorus intake and increasing omega-3 fatty acids are just as important as any protein restriction.

In his book *Unlocking the Canine Ancestral Diet*, Steve Brown points out that the type of fat used in dog food is very important. The ancestors of our dogs ate prey that contained more unsaturated fat in the muscles, marrow, and organs. The meat

DOCTOR'S NOTE

Some dogs have a sensitive pancreas—a lower amount of fat in the diet may help prevent repeated outbreaks of pancreatitis (2 to 3 percent fat in canned food, 8 to 10 percent fat dry food).

of domesticated food animals contains more saturated fat and omega-6 fatty acids, and less omega-3 fatty acids than in the ancestral prey. If the right types of fats are not available, the cells of the body may use less desirable fatty acids and inadvertently impair the function of important high-fat organs, such as the brain. For that reason, dark meats such as chicken thighs and young fryers with most of the skin removed are healthier to home cook with; supplementing with sardines or other sources of unsaturated omega-3 fatty acids is necessary to make up for the lack of them in domesticated food animals and commercial pet food. Adding fresh fatty acids from sardines, flaxseed oil, or fish oil also replaces those fatty acids that became oxidized from the time it took to get from the manufacturing plant to your dog's bowl.

Fat is a great source of fuel and nourishment for the skin and hair coat. The skin's natural oily barrier depends on it. Dogs that eat kibble or dry food with the minimum fat requirements often suffer from dry skin. When those dogs are fed more fat, their skin and coat improves. I've

noticed that their coat odor changes to a musky, healthy smell, and many owners report that they are not as prone to fleas.

Fat is another nutrient with a wide range of percentages in commercial pet foods. The number of calories in a diet largely depends on the amount of fat in the diet, so if you want to reduce the calories, reduce the fat percentage. For example, fast-growing puppies experiencing bone or joint pain may need to eat fewer calories to slow the rapidly growing bones and joints and ease the pain. Another fat- and calorie-related problem is pancreatitis, which may be triggered by high-fat foods, fatty beef scraps, or gluten-filled treats. Feeding small amounts of healthy fat (fish or flax oil) may be a good idea, even when a dog is prone to pancreatitis. You just have to start with very small amounts and increase very gradually.

The chart, above right, from Dog Food Advisor that shows the average fat content of commercial foods and their suggested low-fat percentages.

SUGGESTED LOW-FAT CONTENT PERCENTAGES IN DOG FOOD

Following are the average amounts of fat and low-fat percentages in different types of dog food. It would be hard to find a low-fat raw food appropriate for a weight-challenged dog or a dog with chronic pancreatitis. Feeding those dogs a bit of lean cooked or raw meat may be a better choice.

TYPE	AVERAGE FAT	LOW FAT
Dry	16%	12% or less
Wet	23%	15% or less
Raw	27%	17% or less

CARBOHYDRATE CONTENT

Even though carbohydrates can make up 20 to 70 percent of the nutrients in dog food, they are not essential, because our furry friends can make glucose on their own. So the carbohydrates in the food are broken down to sugar and used for quick energy or stored as fat. You probably won't see the word "carbohydrate" in the guaranteed analysis of the nutrients, but the carbohydrate percentage is easily calculated (see page 83).

The value of carbohydrates in commercial dog foods is often debated. If the carbohydrate comes from whole grains, healthy plants, or vegetables, then its addition is valuable. Grain by-products have lost many of the nutritious components that would make them good ingredients, so they may do little more than increase the amount of poop you have to clean up.

Most commercial foods average 40 to 60 percent carbohydrates, and those are drawn from a variety of potential sources (wheat, rice, corn, barley, oats, potatoes, vegetables, and fruit). Even though most nutritionists are more concerned with the number of calories and the percentage of fat in your dog's diet, the zoologist in me hates to see a high percentage of carbohydrates in a diet for a species that evolved to eat meat and fat. Try to keep

Healthy fat in the diet will improve your dog's coat by improving the skin's natural and protective oil barrier against allergens, bacteria, yeast, and even fleas!

the carbohydrates below 40 percent, but keep in mind that every dog is different and some may do well or even thrive on a high amount of carbs.

Most human and veterinary nutritionists express nutrients as grams per 1,000 calories of food. It isn't difficult to master, but it really does not help you when the guaranteed analysis of most commercial foods isn't measured that way . . . for now. When a food's nutrients (protein, fat, and carbohydrates) are expressed as a percentage of the calories eaten, then the moisture is automatically taken into account. Then you don't have to worry about dry matter and as-fed percentages. The percentage of nutrients per 1,000 calories will be the same for dry, canned, or other commercial foods. Today, only higher-fat foods like raw or all-meat diets are required to be analyzed in this way, because the AAFCO wants to make sure that enough protein and other nutrients are included in the serving size of the higher calorie diet.

Your dog will thank you for a good diet through playfulness, long life, and fewer trips to the vet!

KEY POINTS

1. Know your ingredients. It's better for the ingredient list to contain known animal muscle proteins and fats (like chicken, beef liver, fish, or eggs), vegetables, and fruit. Nongluten whole grains also can be beneficial, if your dog can tolerate them. I always avoid unknown meat meals, animal fats, and meat or grain by-products. The more an ingredient is stripped of its name or vital nutritive parts, the less we can be sure of its quality and where it came from. The combinations of protein, fat, vitamins, and minerals in whole foods are probably better than scientists' best guess on the amounts of essential ingredients to add to nutritionally bankrupt by-products.

2. Quality matters. Some dogs just seem to look and feel better on better quality food. Better quality food has more protein, more fat, better carbohydrate sources, and less synthetic preservatives.

3. Be on the lookout for allergies and sensitivities. If your dog has allergies, you need to find animal and plant proteins that do not cause itching or diarrhea. Avoid wheat gluten, beef, and chicken, to start. Remember: Some synthetic preservatives and thickeners may also add to allergic woes.

4. Different dogs have different needs. A dry or itchy coat needs more healthy fat or oils to nourish it. An obese dog needs fewer calories, higher protein, lower fat, and lower carbohydrates. A higher amount of moisture may help some dogs lose weight or even prevent the formation of crystals that could lead to bladder stones.

5. Say "Yes!" to fewer ingredients. Bathing cells in irritating synthetic or natural substances could lead to inflammation, decreased function, and even cancer. In other words, they may cause unneeded medical issues for our beloved dogs. Avoid controversial synthetic or preservatives and other additives such as BHA, BHT, TBHQ, ethoxyquin, and propylene glycol. Even carrageenan, a natural product, may inflame and irritate the gut in a few sensitive dogs.

6. Moisture is important. It keeps your dog's digestion running smoothly and prevents the formation of urinary crystals and stones.

7. Fat helps keep fur and skin in great shape, but it should come from good sources, and know your dog. If your pup is prone to things like pancreatitis, a low-fat diet may be better.

8. Carbohydrates are debatable and maybe not necessary. Dogs can form their own glucose and don't really need additional carbs from grain by-products, so be wary of foods with lots of low-quality carbs that drive up the calories (not to mention company profits). Carbs from vegetables and fruits may contain needed natural nutrients.

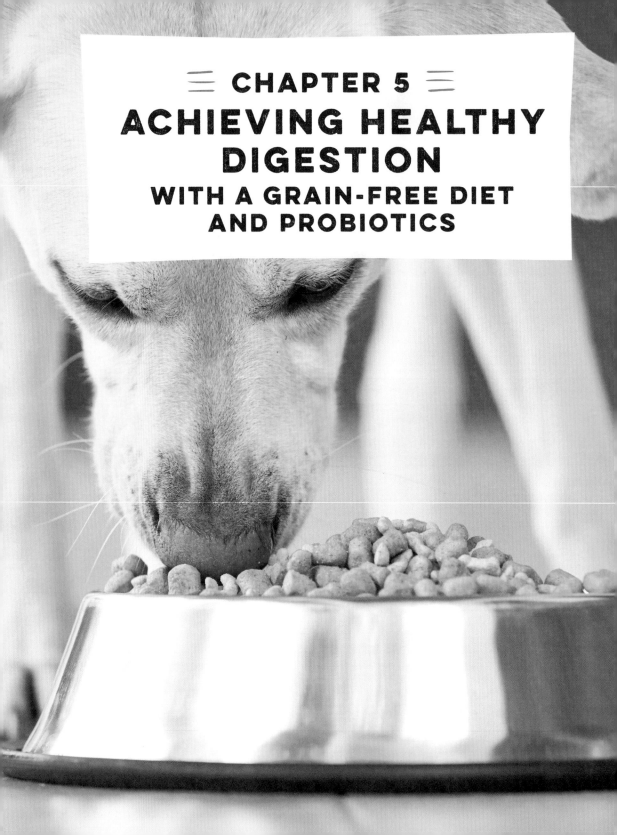

CHAPTER 5

ACHIEVING HEALTHY DIGESTION

WITH A GRAIN-FREE DIET AND PROBIOTICS

Over the last ten years, many pet food companies have created an increasingly wider range of grain-free food and treats. There are four main reasons why grains have become a nutritional enemy in dog food. First, the canine ancestral diet did not contain many grains, yet current economical diets contain an overabundance of them. Second, many owners, and some veterinarians, feel that gluten-containing grains cause allergy-related medical problems in dogs. Third, there is a perception that a high level of grains in dog food may lead to obesity and diabetes. Finally, the grain-free mantra is on everyone's lips and in countless articles. Riding a wave of publicity, the grain-free label is a selling point for dog food.

Does all this mean that grain-free food is better for all dogs? We all know how the pendulum swings in nutritional studies and food mythology. Not so long ago, fat was a nutritional enemy for humans and "low-fat" everything was a steady trend. Now, the general consensus is that related fats (such as polyunsaturated and monounsaturated fatty acids) are not only good for you, but also important. Meanwhile, gluten continues to gain notoriety and is being blamed for all kinds of health issues. Some claims are deserved. After adopting a grain-free diet, many people feel much better, and the diet may cure or help with all types of physical and mental ailments.

Wheat, corn, rice, barley, and oats are the common cereal grains in dog food. The wheat we eat today is quite different from the wheat of the past. Many people believe that the genetic manipulation of the wheat in the 1960s has given it damaging properties. In his book, *Wheat Belly*, author William Davis, MD, explains that the genetically modified gluten of today is a combination of a grain, pesticide, and opiate. Dr. Davis believes that the mutant gluten irritates the lining of the gut to cause digestive problems, and stimulates our hunger, causing weight gain. If gluten does stimulate the appetite, that could explain the reason why some grain-fed dogs act starved all the time.

ANATOMY OF A GRAIN

Whole grain includes the bran, germ, and endosperm containing fiber, vitamins, healthy oils, protein, carbohydrates, minerals, and phytochemicals. The bran and germ are removed when whole grains are processed, leaving the gluten- and carbohydrate-rich endosperm. This is the part of the grain used in economical dog food and treats.

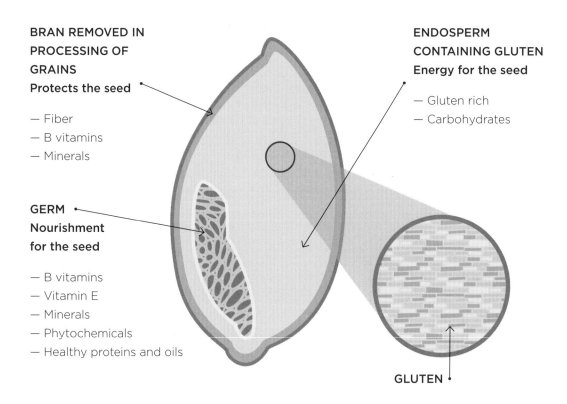

BRAN REMOVED IN PROCESSING OF GRAINS
Protects the seed

— Fiber
— B vitamins
— Minerals

GERM
Nourishment for the seed

— B vitamins
— Vitamin E
— Minerals
— Phytochemicals
— Healthy proteins and oils

ENDOSPERM CONTAINING GLUTEN
Energy for the seed

— Gluten rich
— Carbohydrates

GLUTEN

Where does wheat gluten come from? The wheat kernel, or seed, is the whole grain of the plant. The whole grain consists of germ, bran, and endosperm. When grain is processed, the endosperm (carbohydrate portion) can be separated from the germ and bran layers, thus a large amount of the grain's nutritional value is lost. The carbohydrate-rich endosperm, which naturally contains protein-rich gluten, is then used for everything from baked goods to commercial pet foods. However, the allergenic part of any food is usually the protein.

OTHER ALLERGENS

Just because a label says a diet is for "allergies" or "skin problems" and doesn't include the commonly cited allergens, that isn't a guarantee that the food will cause fewer allergy symptoms in your dog. If your dog shows sensitivity to a food or treat. There is also a common perception that corn is a major allergen in dogs, but it never makes the lists of allergens in the veterinary nutritional literature. The fact is, dogs may be allergic or intolerant to corn—or to any other ingredient in a prescription diet.

A recent advanced nutrition course listed the most common allergens in veterinary medicine as beef, chicken, soy, and dairy. Wheat was not included on the list. Similarly, a 2014 special issue of *Veterinary Clinics of North America: Small Animal Practice* examined clinical nutrition. It lists the top three allergens (in order) as beef, dairy, and wheat. Even though these sources do not list gluten as an allergen, I'm convinced that gluten, or something associated with gluten, in dog food and treats causes a multitude of skin and digestive problems in dogs.

In my practice, hundreds of ear, skin, and digestive problems have cleared up when clients followed a grain-free or limited-ingredient diet regime. When a dog exhibits allergy symptoms, I often counsel the owner to avoid wheat in dog foods, treats, and biscuits—and I've seen many dogs get better when this change is made.

Many dogs can tolerate whole grains or nongluten-containing grains. However, as we already learned, what we feed most pets is not the whole grain with some protein (gluten) and carbs, but instead is an extremely high percentage of gluten—that is what may be triggering the allergic response. Oats and rice are becoming more popular as the gluten grains lose ground. Many limited-ingredient diets for sensitive dogs include these grains in a variety of combinations such as chicken and rice, lamb and rice, salmon and rice, turkey and oats, or kangaroo and oats.

Even these gluten-free grain combinations may still be troublesome for some dogs. One of my patients had been to several vets and had vomited on and off for seven years, until rice was taken out of the diet. She was allergic to beef, salmon, wheat, barley, and . . . rice! She did much better on chicken, chicken liver, eggs, peas, and carrots—and she stopped vomiting within a few weeks.

My success with treating allergic patients has reinforced my position that exposure to wheat may be an important factor in triggering allergic reactions. If the food contained other allergens or processing chemicals that caused the problem, then the course of action still remains the same. If your dog is itchy, inflamed, or sick, I suggest you steer clear of inexpensive food as well as food and treats made with wheat and barley.

KEEPING CARBOHYDRATES IN MIND

It's no secret that grain-free diets have become popular as advertising and public demand push sales higher. However, gluten sensitivities aren't the only reason grain-free foods are promoted for better health. We previously talked about the ancestral diet of the wolf: A predator's diet is usually a mix of moister, higher-protein, higher-fat, and lower-carbohydrate ingredients than those found in most commercial foods. Even if today's dogs have adapted to having some grain in their diet, too much grain and carbohydrates may contribute to increasing obesity, diabetes, and joint problems that are so common in our pets.

Because the ancestral diet of our pets did not contain a high percentage of carbohydrate, or as many grain and grain by-products as commercial diets, people often assume that grain-free diets automatically have a lower amount of carbohydrates and, therefore, are better for obese pets. This may or may not be true, depending on the calorie count of the ingredients in question, as grains are often replaced with potatoes and other starchy foods, which add carbohydrate calories to the mix. If your dog is inactive and gains weight easily, a lower-fat and lower-carbohydrate diet may help him lose weight. Just keep in mind that a grain-free diet is not an instant guarantee the diet is a low-carbohydrate one.

PROBIOTICS, PREBIOTICS, AND THE IMMUNE SYSTEM

I bet you didn't know that there are more bacteria living in and on us than there are cells in our body. Adding probiotics (good bacteria) to the diet has proven beneficial for digestive health.

The general consensus is that probiotics do their work in several ways. The friendly bacteria work to crowd out the bad bacteria, and the by-products of their fermentation may help the immune system and the cells of the intestine work more effectively against invaders. This modulation by bacterial fermentation products, like short-chain fatty acids, may nourish the cells of the intestine and help the immune system focus on the problem, instead of causing inflammation and escalating the problem.

So how do you choose a probiotic for your dog? Probiotics can be confusing because there seem to be as many products as there are bacteria. The general rule is: The more bacteria per serving, the better. There are products that contain anywhere from a paltry 10 million CFU bacteria to a robust 500 billion CFU bacteria per dose. For severe cases of chronic diarrhea or urinary tract infections, I recommend at least 5 billion CFU bacteria daily. Smaller levels, from 100 million CFU to 5 billion CFU bacteria per dose, may help treat milder issues, prevent infections, and keep the digestive tract happy and healthy.

Consider adding probiotic powder or capsules to your dog's diet to help boost beneficial gut bacteria.

Many commercial dog foods now use low levels of probiotics in their diets, and any amount of healthy bacteria is probably better than none. I used to recommend yogurt for the probiotic effects but found that most yogurt has low levels of bacteria and may be less effective than probiotic powder or capsules (available online or at the drugstore). Additionally, some dogs are intolerant to dairy products; you would have to feed 4 ounces of yogurt daily for them to receive enough of the good bacteria, which might lead to GI distress.

So what are prebiotics? Prebiotics are types of fermentable fiber that your dog's gut bacteria feed on. Those bacteria then release healthy by-products for the host. When yeast ferment sugar, grapes, or hops they release alcohol as a by-product, whereas yeast in bread dough release carbon dioxide, making the dough rise. The bacteria and yeast in your dog's gut eat the fiber, release healthful compounds that feed the cells of your dog's intestine, and may help the immune system reduce inflammation and prevent infection. When certain soluble plant fibers are fermented, healthful products may increase. When those types of fiber are mixed in with the food, or are included in the diet, the benefits are increased. Prebiotic fibers are eaten by the friendly probiotic bacteria, which produce healthy compounds for your dog.

Fructo-oligosaccharides (FOS), inulin (a prebiotic used in digestive supplements), and oligofructose are common prebiotics that are good fuel for those healthy by-products. You'll see beet pulp and guar gum in the ingredient lists; they are examples of prebiotic types of fiber ingredients used in commercial food.

Probiotics, or even prebiotics, may be a good idea for some dogs with chronic medical issues or a more sensitive gut, but probiotics will not make your dog's diet more healthful or less allergenic. If your dog has medical issues that your vet thinks may be caused by food ingredients, change the food to a limited-ingredient or novel-protein diet first, and then use probiotics (check the label for one that is more than 5 billion CFU daily).

KEY POINTS

1. Feeding grains such as oats and rice, and avoiding gluten grains (wheat and barley), may be the answer for your gluten-sensitive dog. As people seek out more gluten-free foods for themselves, they also turn to gluten-free foods for their pets. Grain-free diets are gaining popularity because gluten grains can cause skin, ear, and bowel discomfort in sensitive dogs. Some dogs can tolerate whole grains, but many commercial foods contain processed grains with exceptionally high levels of gluten by-products. This may be the culprit causing medical issues.

2. Incorporate vegetables, fruit, and whole grains in your dog's diet. When it comes to carbohydrates, look to vegetables and fruit—they are much more healthful sources than grain by-products because they also contain healthful antioxidants and vitamins. For nutrients, seek out nongluten whole grains.

3. Keeping your dog healthy starts with a healthy diet and healthy gut. Maintaining a robust, bacterial community in the gut protects your dog from infections and diarrhea as well as other medical issues. Giving your dog a daily dose of probiotic capsules or powder helps nourish the cells of the intestinal tract. The billions of healthful bacteria in probiotics may also help with bowel problems, stress during trips or boarding, or even bladder problems.

CHAPTER 6
PUPPY DIETS

Puppies eat more often than fully grown dogs. They also require twice the calories and nutrients to nourish their growing bodies until their growth rate slows down. Because their bodies are under construction, raw materials are needed in slightly larger quantities for their size to build all the necessary muscles, bones, joints, organs, and destructive teeth.

Traditional puppy-diet kibbles are smaller, contain more protein, and have an evenly balanced calcium/phosphorus ratios for growing bodies. Protein and minerals, such as calcium and phosphorus, provide the "bricks and mortar" for the frame that houses their important organs. If the materials for the framework are not available in the right proportions, then faulty construction of joints may result, which can lead to wear and tear of the cartilage and arthritis. Puppy food is usually fed to match most the puppy's high rate of growth from three to six months of age. After that, the growth rate slows, fewer calories and nutrients are needed, and the larger teeth and jaws can easily handle adult dog food.

BONE AND JOINT GROWTH

Puppy food is a good idea, but not absolutely necessary for some mixed-breed dogs. That's a good thing for families with dogs of various ages. We all know that no matter what you try to feed one pet, the other one wants it. The puppy will always want some of the adult food and vice versa. To be on the safe side, you can buy "all life-stages" dog food and feed it to everybody. Most small-breed and mixed-breed puppies will thrive on a variety of adult foods, raw food, and homemade food, provided that the correct amount of bone meal is added.

It's important to note that the same is not true for those breeds that experience explosive growth. Imagine a bricklayer trying to do a job without having the bricks needed to build a strong wall. The same thing happens when rapidly growing puppies are fed an imbalanced diet. Bones and joints are made of minerals, such as calcium, phosphorous, and magnesium, that give the surrounding protein fibers their strength. Those mineral deposits and proteins (called collagens) are laid down by the puppy's bone cells according to the genetic plans. As you might guess, the sizes and shapes of the various joints are really important. Hip, shoulder, and elbow joints are individually contoured to fit the architecture defined in each puppy's genes. Whether it be a ball-and-socket (like the hip) or hinged (like the elbow) joints are lined with smooth, slippery cartilage and joint lubricant to glide effortlessly and without any friction.

DOCTOR'S NOTE

As puppies, large-breed dogs experience the highest growth rates. Their bones and joints are under tremendous stress and may not develop correctly if they don't get the right nutrition.

In fast-growing puppies without the correct balance of important nutrients, the rate of growth prevents the bone and cartilage cells from doing their best work. This process may be hampered by a lack of, or abundance of, calcium or suffer because the bones are lengthening faster than the remodeling cells can cope with.

Bone problems collectively called "developmental orthopedic diseases" can occur in young, fast-growing dogs. Any rapidly growing puppy can be prone to painful bones and joints, but these particular issues are more common in German shepherds, Dobermans, Newfoundlands, Bernese mountain dogs, golden retrievers, Saint Bernards, Great Danes, bassett hounds, and Labradors. These fast-growing puppies can double and triple their weight in just a month or two. Bone and joint problems resulting from this rapid rate of growth can range from mild self-limiting ones, such as panosteitis, when the bones and joints become inflamed, to other more severe problems resulting from poorly shaped joints.

For example, the ball and socket of the hip joint may be poorly shaped so the lining of the joint suffers as those surfaces rub together. Friction from a loose or tight fit can wear down the cartilage covering of the socket or the ball. Once this occurs, pain and arthritis can set in at an early age. Then the joint is labeled with the medical term "dysplasia," meaning abnormal growth or development. Mild lameness may progress to moderate or severe lameness with age. It is really hard to know what the future holds. The radiographs of some dogs may show horrible arthritic changes in the joints, and the dog will limp only occasionally, while other radiographs will show only mild changes but the dog exhibits severe lameness. It's all in how the body compensates and shields itself or deals with the pain.

Growing too fast is a result of selective breeding for a larger size. That's why these joint problems occur in certain breeds of dogs. Giant-breed puppies born weighing 1 pound (455 g) can easily

Your puppy needs a complete diet so his quickly growing muscles, joints, and bones form properly.

gain 150 pounds (68 kg) within the first 18 months of life. Not only that, but some large-breed puppies can keep growing until they are 2 years of age, meaning their bones are under construction for a year longer than smaller breeds of dogs. This rapid rate of growth and long "growing season" can wreak havoc with the architectural plan for the bones and joints. It is possible, however, that these poorly constructed joints or cartilage coverings may be part of the genetic plan and, therefore, can't be avoided, even with a better diet.

Consider a large-breed puppy formula for breeds such as a St. Bernard. Large breeds need fewer calories and the proper balance of calcium and phosphorus. Staying on the lean side may prevent bone or joint problems leading to life-long painful arthritis.

AVOIDING JOINT PROBLEMS IN GROWING PUPPIES

Nutrition has long been suspected to have something to do with developmental orthopedic problems in puppies. The high rate of growth in large- and giant-breed puppies makes them extremely prone to excesses or deficiencies of calcium or phosphorus. When the bones are growing at such a rapid rate, too much or too little calcium may cause imperfections that result in joints and cartilage that wear out much too soon. I hardly ever see problems with underfeeding large-breed puppies, but overfeeding them may create serious problems, as overweight puppies develop bone and joint problems more often than lean ones. Any fast-growing pup that is gaining too much weight (a body condition score of more than 5 out of 9, see page 140) or exhibiting symptoms of joint pain should be fed less, changed to a lower calorie food, or started on a large-breed puppy formula until they are 12 months old.

Giant-breed puppies may need food with fewer calories (less than 3,500 calories per kilogram of food and less than 15 percent fat), a lower calcium-to-phosphorus ratio (close to 1.2:1), and lower percentage of calcium (around 1 percent). These large-breed puppy diets—not just puppy food!—have been formulated to help slow down the growth rate and ensure proper bone and joint nourishment. If a large-breed puppy has really big joints and is growing fast, he needs to stay on the lean side, with a body condition score of 3–4 out of 9 (see page 140). He also should eat one of the large-breed puppy diets for the first year of his life.

A puppy's food should be measured out and fed twice daily; not just scooped and left out for the puppy to free feed on. High-calorie treats should be avoided. The

DOCTOR'S NOTE

When you want a dog to gain or lose weight without switching its food, start by adjusting the amount fed by 20 percent in the appropriate direction—20 percent more to help the puppy to gain, 20 percent less to encourage weight loss.

puppy's ability to control the amount of calcium that ends up in the blood is not developed until after 6 months. If a puppy is fed extra calcium (in the form of raw bones, bone meal, calcium tablets, or calcium supplements) during his high-growth phase, typically from 3 to 6 months, the probability of a bone or joint problem dramatically increases. So it is up to you to manage your puppy's calcium intake.

There is tremendous variation in the growth rate of dogs. Some puppies and genetic lines may grow faster and need more help than others, while other large-breed puppies are smaller and have a reasonable growth rate. The decision to feed a regular puppy formula, large-breed puppy formula, or all life stages depends on the growth rate, size of the joints, or development of any growing pains in the long bones. If that happens, get recommendations from your vet.

Consider feeding the large-breed puppy diet to a giant-breed puppy, any other breed that has big joints or a puppy that is growing fast.

Large-breed puppies may develop panosteitis or bone pain from rapid growth. Vets check for bone pain by squeezing on the bones above the elbow, knee, and hock of the pup. Many pups hate this anyway, but if a dog has bone pain, he is liable to yelp when gentle pressure is applied to the middle or ends of the long bones. (Check out my YouTube video showing how to check your large-breed puppy for joint pain at http://youtu.be/muq4XbHlMZl.) If a pup starts to develop bone pain, most vets prescribe a course of anti-inflammatory drugs and may advise feeding less food or changing to a large-breed diet. It is also common for this bone pain to be very mild, self-limiting, and to disappear in several weeks without any dietary changes.

DOCTOR'S NOTE

Large, thick, evenly rolled chews are needed for most puppies, or they are immediately eaten. Try to buy domestically made products that are free of tanning chemicals or preservatives. Chicken jerky strips and other treats made in China may be linked to kidney problems and even death in dogs. All treats made in China should be avoided until the cause is known.

Chewing is a normal activity, and most pet stores have a variety of choices for this purpose. To be safe, purchase only rawhide chews made domestically.

HOW MUCH TO FEED A GROWING PUPPY

The good news is you can usually follow the recommendations on the can, bag, or box. In fact, that will work well for most small and medium breed puppies. Most puppies don't have the growth issues that we discussed in the previous section, but if yours does, it's important to take it seriously.

Always keep in mind that package directions and formulas are averages.

Your puppy may need more or less food, depending on its activity level and individual metabolism (how well it burns calories). If the puppy gains weight too fast, or seems to be losing weight, then the amount fed can be adjusted.

Let's say you want to cut down the amount of his food because your puppy is getting too fat. If you were feeding 10 ounces (283 g) of food twice daily or 20 ounces (567 g) total daily, you would decrease the amount by 20 percent, which equals 4 ounces (113 g). You would,

Keeping your puppy on the lean side is important, especially in large breed dogs such as Labradors that are prone to obesity.

therefore, feed 16 ounces (453 g) for weight loss and 24 ounces (680 g) for weight gain daily. While 4 ounces doesn't seem like much, when the average dry food is about 40 to 50 calories per ounce, then that is a 160 calorie difference per day. If you are feeding a large-breed puppy or want to know exactly how many calories to consider feeding, consult the Daily Calories chart in appendix C, on page 181. It includes the calories needed for various life stages in dogs. The number of calories per kilogram, pound, or can, lets you know how many ounces to feed a day.

Keeping your dogs on the lean side and measuring food may prevent medical issues later. Studies have shown that puppies and dogs fed free choice had a much higher incidence of developing arthritis and developmental orthopedic diseases. Being overweight has an adverse effect on your pet's life. Diseases associated with being overweight may rob them of 1.8 years. In human years (at 4 to 5 dog years per human year), that's equivalent to 8 human years!

Small-breed or mixed-breed puppies are not nearly as prone to all these joint and growth problems as large-breed dogs. Regardless, it remains important to keep them on the thin side. Monitoring weight in puppies and adults can add both years and comfort to a dog's life.

OTHER HAZARDS FOR PUPPIES

Puppies are prone to stomach and bowel upset from sampling just about any item lying around the house or yard. They will chew clothes, shoes, plants, ant traps, wood, plastic, foil, electric cords, dead critters, snail bait, and any number of things that will get them in trouble. Puppies consider anything within their reach a chew toy or food. Depending on their height and ability, anything may fall victim to their curiosity. As puppies explore their environment, they will also be exposed to bacteria, cysts, and spores. Depending on the pup's immune system and the object, bacteria, or parasite ingested, some may vomit, get a mild case of the runs, or even prolonged bowel upsets. This is a normal, self-limiting condition for many pups. However, moderate to severe vomiting or diarrhea can lead to dehydration and shock in young pups, so monitor the severity closely.

Some puppies, if they are allergic to beef protein, may react to the beef skin with diarrhea, hives, red ears, or even seizures. Large, raw bones are a good choice for recreational chewing by puppies, as long as the bones are big enough that the puppy can't break them into pieces and eat them. The hope is they will gnaw on large bones or rawhide instead of our possessions.

In the same vein, a puppy's intestinal tract can be taught to better digest a variety of foods. If a puppy or adult dog is fed the same exact diet all the time, his intestine and bacterial flora gets used to the ingredients and levels of nutrients. A change in dog food, treats, or snagging a piece of human food may confuse an uneducated gut and make it crampy or loose. If a puppy's gut gets used to different ingredients, then changes may not be so apt to lead to smelly or messy results.

Depending on your puppy's breed and growth characteristics, a puppy diet or "all life stages" with excellent ingredients and a protein level above 25 to 30 percent is ideal. Then, depending on what is for dinner, a piece or two of a healthy lean meat, fish, or vegetable can be added to the food. I've followed this example, and my dogs rarely have issues with changes in their diet, or, if they do, it is usually just a soft or slightly slimy stool. Small changes over time will help the digestion system adapt to larger changes in less time. It will take time for those lessons to be learned and to achieve a more tolerant digestive system in your puppy. Remember to always introduce new foods and treats in small amounts over several days to make sure the pup tolerates the pup tolerates the new ingredients.

KEY POINTS

1. Keep all puppies on the lean side (4–5 out of 9 on the body condition system (BCS) chart). See page 140.

2. Feed puppy formula, large-breed puppy formula, or all life-stages formula depending on the puppy's growth rate, size of their joints, and expected adult size.

3. Introduce new food over a 4- to 5-day period and expect all puppies to have a soft stool or vomit on occasion. Diarrhea and soft stool in puppies can be normal or a sign of medical problems. If the vomiting of diarrhea looks dangerous or worsens, have your pup checked for parasites or parvovirus.

≡ CHAPTER 7 ≡
FEEDING THE ACTIVE OR ATHLETIC DOG

Active dogs have different dietary requirements than sedentary dogs due to their high levels of energy and metabolism. Athletic dogs like to push themselves and need better fuel and ingredients to keep them healthy, happy, and injury free.

Let's pretend you own a super active, Jack Russell Terrier that runs the perimeter of the yard checking on everything. Would you say he burns more calories than a racing greyhound? How would your little terrier rank against a hunting dog or a search-and-rescue dog? How about compared to a dock diver, agility, or sled dog?

If you guessed that you'll need more information to answer these questions, you're right. The calories expended depend on the level of the exertion and the time spent doing the activity. Let's compare the time spent on these different activities.

The more time a dog spends on the move, the more calories he expends. Constant activity such as hours of running, hunting, or searching, use up far more fuel than sprinting or diving for shorter periods of time. Your Jack Russell's daily activities, therefore, burn far more calories than a greyhound's day at the track—and possibly as many as a spaniel or pointer on the hunt for birds.

Dogs have evolved for long-distance and aerobic exercise. In nature programs, we see wolves chase down prey, running at moderate speed over long distances. This ability is part of our dogs' genetic makeup. Their muscles and biochemistry are geared to efficiently burn fat for fuel. When they engage in high-intensity exercise for a brief period of time, such as sprinting, they depend on glycogen in the muscles, while moderate activity over a longer period of time depends on protein and fat to replenish the glycogen and fuel the muscle. This allows them to efficiently use fat as fuel more quickly and over a range of effort.

Athletic dogs that spend lots of time on the move need to eat more food and calories, but they should stay on the lean side so that their own body weight does not add more stress to the workload. Leaner dogs stay healthier and suffer fewer injuries. (Very cold weather also increases the need for more calories, as the body burns fat and protein to keep warm.)

Seeing the smooth outline of the ribs and a tuck of the abdomen into the flank is a healthy sign. Monitor the back muscles that run on both sides of the spine. If a dog that is working hard is being fed too few calories or not enough protein, the ribs will be evident, the spine will stick up more, and the muscles alongside the spine will flatten out. That would occur only if a dog was really burning the calories, running for hours, and not eating enough fuel. It could also occur if a dog was not digesting or absorbing her food. Special blood tests would show if that is the case.

ACTIVE DOGS AND ENDURANCE LEVELS

A greyhound accelerates to 35 miles (56 km) per hour, and a typical race lasts 30 seconds. The rest of the day is spent resting in a kennel or in a larger run.

The sled dogs' stamina and endurance is legendary. These amazing wolflike dogs need to keep warm, pull a sled, and run for hours. The level of exertion in hunting can vary widely.

Your neighbor's Lab spends weekends at the duck club where he waits for the command to "fetch" and will dutifully retrieve the fallen bird. He may fetch for hours or much less time, depending on the number of birds and the hunter's accuracy.

Other bird dogs will cover lots of ground at a moderate to frantic pace over several hours flushing out quail or pheasants.

Search-and-rescue dogs will work for hours looking for lost or injured people.

The body condition system (BCS) developed by Purina is an easy way to monitor your dog's weight (see page 140). As we'll talk about in chapter 9 on obesity, this system is a way of looking at your dog's body to assess the amount of fat he has and score it on a range from 1 to 9.

A score of 1 indicates severely underweight whereas a score of 9 indicates severely overweight. Most people think a dog that is at the right weight is too thin, because that athletic dog sticks out in a population of dogs that are on the high end of the scale (6–9 range).

A dock diver will accelerate and jump for distance, but only minutes are spent on the jump and swim back.

The Jack Russell burns lots of calories listening, barking, running, and working himself into a frenzy over the orange tabby cat that sits on the fence and stares at him.

DOCTOR'S NOTE

At rest and during exercise, dogs burn twice as much energy from fat as humans do.

Once you learn to use the BCS and calorie chart, you can increase or decrease the amount of food in your active dog's diet depending on the activity and BCS of your dog. To begin, use the activity and calorie chart in appendix C to determine how much to feed your dog, or refer to the feeding directions on your pet's food for the recommended amount of food. Then monitor your dog's BCS to decide if the amount of food needs adjustment. If your dog's BCS falls below a score of 4, increase the amount of food by 20 percent (see page 125 in the previous chapter for more on this).

A dog that is involved with agility, Frisbee or disc, coursing, flyball, dock jumping, or greyhound racing may only need 10 to 20 percent more calories than the average dog. Many may not need an increase in calories at all; instead, a good-quality commercial mix of ingredients will do. A herding, hunting, search-and-rescue, or field trial dog may need more calories, as well, depending on time spent being active. Most commercially available food with higher protein and fat will be suitable for a moderately active dog. If a dog consistently spends up to 3 hours working, training, or playing, she may need a food higher in protein and fat.

GUARANTEED ANALYSIS FOR ACTIVE DOGS

The guaranteed analysis in dry and canned food for hardworking dogs engaged in strenuous activities may look like this. It includes more protein than the average diet and more fat than the low-fat diet.

NUTRIENT	DRY FOOD	CANNED FOOD
Protein	30%	8%
Fat	25%	7%
Fiber	5%	2%
Ash	6%	1%
Moisture	10%	75%

For those dogs that consistently spend more than 3 hours per day exercising, more protein and fat may be needed to help maintain their weight. High-calorie diets have more fat and less fiber. The high-calorie sled-dog diet may contain 40 percent protein, 50 to 60 percent fat, and very little carbohydrate and fiber. A hardworking dog deserves the best fuel you can afford. Consider adding cooked or raw lean meat, eggs, sardines, or raw food to the menu to ensure quality protein for maintenance of the tendons, muscles, and joints. A 3.75-ounce (106 g) tin of sardines in water or olive oil is a great supplement that you can easily add to any commercial or homemade food several times a week. It's a good idea to give all active dogs a daily joint supplement such as glucosamine condroitin daily to nourish their hardworking joings.

KEY POINTS

1. Dogs involved in strenuous activities need more and higher-quality food to service their hard working machines. In addition to buying a higher-quality food, consider supplementing 10 to 20 percent of the diet with several ounces of meat, eggs, fish, liver, and beef heart. Adding frozen or freeze-dried raw food to the menu is an easy way to increase the amount of protein and fat in the diet.

2. Remember: Athletic dogs don't need to lug extra weight around. Keep your dog on the lean side, especially if the dog is involved in strenuous activities.

CHAPTER 8
CANINE OBESITY

PERHAPS THE MOST COMMON THING I HEAR IN MY PRACTICE IS, "WHY DOES MY DOG GET SO HEAVY? HE HARDLY EATS ANYTHING!" Half of the dogs in the United States are overweight. You might not think that an overweight dog is a big deal, but there is a variety of conditions that are much more present in obese dogs than in leaner ones. Extra pounds can make a dog's life more difficult, dangerous, and painful.

OBESITY MAY CAUSE OR LEAD TO

— Anesthetic or surgical complications

— Reduced lifespan of, on average, 1.8 years (8 human years)

— Reduced quality of life due to an inability to move around, decreased energy, or feeling bad from other medical conditions caused by extra weight

— A poor immune system, leaving the body more prone to infections

— Diabetes and the need for insulin injections for life

— Pancreatitis (the tendency for the pancreas to become inflamed and painful), which could mean a low-fat or prescription diet for life

— Painful joint problems such as arthritis, developmental orthopedic diseases, degenerative joint problems, hip dysplasia, osteoarthritis, chronic lameness and pain, torn cruciate ligament of the stifle, back problems

— Breathing and heart problems from belly fat pushing on the throat, diaphragm, chest, and vessels

— Chronic cough and even tracheal collapse

— Heatstroke due to increased insulation that prevents cooling

— Cancer, especially mammary and urinary (bladder)

— Low thyroid levels in the blood requiring lifelong thyroid medication

In 2013, Veterinary Pet Insurance policyholders filed more than $17 million in claims for conditions and diseases that are caused, all or in part, by obesity. In a 2005 study, it was estimated that 42 percent of dogs aged 5 to 11 years old were overweight. That gives your dog a good chance of being over his ideal weight. Fortunately, as we'll learn, for most dogs, being overweight is an easily reversible condition when you know the ingredients in your dog's food and treats, and the right amount of each to feed.

The body condition system (BCS) makes it possible to determine the proper size for your dog. It ranks a dog's body based on the amount of fat that covers his ribs, back, and base of tail. After reading the description, studying the chart seen on page 140, and with a bit of practice, you should be able to put your dog in one of the numbered categories to identify his BCS score.

Is your dog overweight? So many factors can produce this condition, but regardless of the cause, this ailment can have dangerous effects on a dog's health and longevity.

CLASSIFYING YOUR DOG USING THE BODY CONDITION SYSTEM (BCS)

TOO THIN

1. Lumbar vertebrae, pelvic bones, and ribs are visibly noticeable. No evidence of body fat. Distinct lack of muscle tone.

2. Lumbar vertebrae, pelvic bones, and ribs are visibly noticeable. Nominal lack of muscle mass.

3. Ribs easily visibly noticeable with no visible fat. Lumbar vertebrae visible and pelvic bones slightly noticeable.

IDEAL

4. Minimal fat covering ribs. Waist easily visibly discernible. Abdominal tuck is distinct.

5. Minimal fat covering ribs. Waist behind ribs evident when viewed from overhead. Abdomen tucks up when viewed from the side.

TOO HEAVY

6. Ribs palpably discernible but with some excess fat. Waist is noticeable when viewed from overhead, but not prominent. Abdominal tuck is visible.

7. Ribs somewhat palpably discernible but with heavy fat covering. Fat deposits obvious over base of tail and lumbar area. Waist undetectable or barely visible. Some abdominal tuck can be seen.

8. Ribs only palpably detectable with considerable pressure. Heavy fat deposits obvious over base of tail and lumbar area. Waist visibly undetectable. No abdominal tuck. Distention of the abdomen may be present.

9. Massive fat deposits between the neck, abdomen, spine, and base of tail. Waist visibly undetectable. Obvious distention of the abdomen.

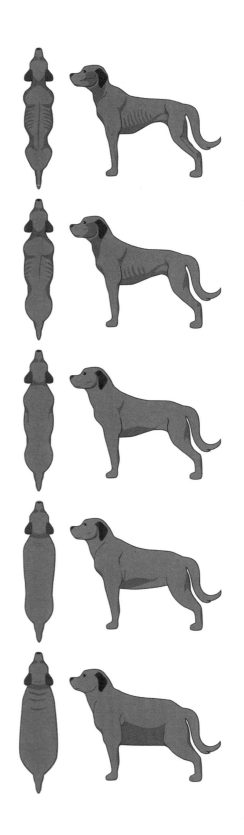

A BCS score of 5 is the ideal weight. The ribs can be felt through a slight fat covering. You can see the waist—the indented area behind the ribs—from above. From the side, the abdomen is "tucked up."

Even with this handy chart, studies have shown that it is hard for most pet owners to judge their pet's weight. Many owners believe a BCS of 5 is much too thin and would choose the picture corresponding to a body condition score of 6 or 7 as the perfect weight. The truth of the BCS might surprise you. A loving owner may visualize a loving pet as a slightly plump 7, when it is actually a 9. Your vet, family members, or friends may be able to help you use the chart to accurately assess your pet's weight.

It's much easier for me to evaluate a dog's BCS, because I look at many dogs daily and get a good perspective on the various sizes, breeds, body types, and how the fat is usually distributed over the body. The weight assessment may be more difficult for those not used to looking at and feeling different types of dogs. Some dogs hide their chunkiness beneath fur. Others are quite "boxy" or "squatty" and hard to evaluate.

Once your dog is assigned a body condition score, you can easily calculate how much weight your dog needs to lose. Let's follow a real-life example: Pat's brings her chubby, six-year-old Pomeranian, Penny, for a visit to the veterinary hospital.

Penny used to weigh 11 pounds (5 kg), but she started to gain weight after she was spayed. Over the course of 3 years, her weight climbed to 18 pounds (8.2 kg). Penny's knees and back seemed to be causing her pain, and at her annual checkup, Penny's veterinarian advised weight loss to solve these issues. She also advised Pat to have Penny's blood checked to make sure that her thyroid was functioning properly and that her other organs were working well.

After her vet's recommendation, Pat was determined to help Penny lose some weight. She looked at the BCS chart to determine the amount of weight Penny needed to lose. Pat couldn't easily feel her pet's ribs, and there were large fat deposits in the rib and tail areas. When Penny's hair was wet down, Pat could see that there was no indentation behind the ribs and that the belly was distended a bit beyond the level of the ribs.

Pat evaluated that Penny's score should be an 8, because the belly was not too distended. From the side, Penny's belly did not tuck into the flanks, but horizontally continued to the back legs. Pat could feel the "fat pad" of the belly and the bulge of the abdomen and decided Penny could be edging toward a 9. Pat finally settled on a body condition score of 8.5.

Lean meats such as fish and chicken are great sources of protein for an overweight dog.

If we divide Penny's weight by that figure of 135 percent, we will arrive at the ideal weight for a leaner Penny. Remember that we said Penny weighs 18 pounds (8 kg), so 18 ÷ 1.35 = 13.5, so an ideal weight of 13.5 pounds (6 kg). If we subtract the ideal weight of 13.5 pounds (6 kg) from the present weight of 18 pound (8 kg), painful Penny should lose 4.5 pounds (2 kg) over a few months to help her feel better and become more mobile. Just 4.5 pounds (2 kg) is 25 percent of her body weight, which is a lot of extra weight to be hauling around on sore, inflamed joints.

Studies show that a weekly weight loss of .5 percent to 2 percent of body weight is safe for most dogs. To make it simpler, let's use a weekly weight loss of 1 percent of body weight. In Penny's case, 18 pounds (8 kg) times 1 percent equals 0.18 pounds (8 g), which we can round up to 0.2 pounds (90 g) of planned weight loss per week. That is 0.8 pounds (362 g) per month. If Penny lost 0.8 pounds (362 g) per month, it would take her 5.5 months, or about 6 months, to go from a BCS of 8.5 to one of a 5 or 6. The weight should be monitored every week or so. Then the amount of food or type of food can be adjusted for more or less weight loss.

As with all weight loss, it's not as important to lose weight in a specific time period as it is to consistently move toward the ideal weight. Six months is a good time frame goal, but more time may be needed. In Penny's case, we may want to make her more comfortable in a

Each number over the ideal weight of 5 on the body condition score chart adds 10 percent to the amount Penny is overweight. So, if we used a BCS of 8.5 to calculate Penny's ideal weight, she would be 35 percent over the ideal (8.5 – 5 = 3.5. 3.5 × 10 = 35%). In other words, if a BCS of 5 is ideal for 100 percent of the dog's weight, Penny is 135 percent of her ideal weight.

HOW MUCH WEIGHT DOES YOUR DOG NEED TO LOSE?

To figure this out, identify your dog's BCS:

For each number over a BCS of 5, your dog is 10 percent overweight. So if your dog has a BCS of 7, you figure 7 – 5 = 2 and 2 × 10 = 20% over ideal weight.

Divide your dog's current weight by (100 + the percent over ideal weight) to get to the ideal weight. Continuing the example, if your dog's BCS is 7, and his current weight is 86 pounds (39 kg), you would divide the current weight by 120 percent (86 ÷ 1.20) to get to 71.6 pounds (32 kg). Or, to round up, 72 pounds (33 kg).

Subtract the ideal weight from the current weight to get to the number of pounds your dog needs to shed: current weight (86) – ideal weight (72) = pounds to be shed (14).

An average ideal weight-loss goal is 1 percent of body weight is safe for dogs. In this example, 86 pounds × 0.01 = 0.86 pounds (0.39 kg) weight loss per week. Let's round up to 1 pound (0.5 kg).

To calculate the weight-loss timeframe, divide the weight per week into the total pounds to lose. In this example, 14 pounds (6.3 kg) to lose at 1 pound (0.5 kg) per week is 14 weeks, or 3.5 months.

little less time by losing a bit more weight per month. Gradual weight loss of 3 to 4 pounds (1.4 to 1.8 kg) per month could help Penny feel better faster and avoid many issues associated with those extra pounds.

When Penny's blood was tested, her thyroid panel showed that the level of thyroxin (the active thyroid molecule that regulates her metabolism), was low.

Penny's veterinarian determined that a thyroid pill could be given twice daily to see if that would help Penny lose weight, as well as help her thin, light-colored hair coat. Because Penny's blood work showed that her organs were in good shape. Her vet decided that a mild NSAID, or pain reliever, might allow her to walk a bit more easily, which would help her burn some extra calories. Along with the thyroid pill

Keep in mind how often you offer treats to your pet and how nutritious they are. If your dog needs to lose weight, where can you cut back?

and pain pills, she prescribed a decrease in food and treats in Penny's diet, as well as some additional activity for Penny to lose weight.

So what is the quantity of food that Pat should feed Penny to help her lose weight? How do we know how much kibble or dry food, canned food, dehydrated food, or home-cooked food to feed our pets? Take a look at the Daily Calories chart in appendix C (page 181) that shows the resting and maintenance energy requirements of adult dogs. This chart will show you how much food and the different calories needed for a resting

dog, a normally active dog, a young dog, an inactive dog, and an active older dog. Pat and her vet looked at this same chart.

The chart calculates calories per day by using a formula of weight in kilograms to the three-quarter power. This seems complicated, but, for the purposes of this book, you just need to know that this formula is more accurate because the weight and calories burned follow a pattern used from analyzing many different species and their weights.

In the chart, active dogs are those that may spend 1 or more hours running, walking, or playing—dogs who naturally like to move. Continuing with our example, Pat followed the chart from row 18 pounds (8 kg) to the inactive column, which is for middle-aged with a sedentary lifestyle. It showed that Penny needed around 437 calories per day to keep her going. The vet helped Pat find a low-fat, no grain, senior diet that might help Penny lose some weight. Pat decided she would buy a few cans of the low-fat chicken and veggies and transition Penny to the new food over a week's time, as her vet suggested. Half of a 12-ounce (340 g) can twice daily adds up to 380 calories, or 32 calories per ounce (28 g), which left some room for several small pieces of lean chicken from Pat's dinner plate.

Penny's vet told Pat that another simple rule of thumb is to decrease the amount of kibble, canned food, human table food, biscuits, dental chews, or other treats eaten daily by 20 percent. To do that, a dog owner has to take *all* food and treats into account. Every food item's contained calories and has to be cut by 20 percent.

After reviewing everything, Pat adjusted Penny's diet. Penny now enjoyed one-quarter cup or a few ounces of reduced-calorie dry food daily and one-half can of wet food twice daily. She also earned two to three small treats daily for being a loving companion and obeying the rules. This included lean meats shared from Pat's dinner, which were also subject to the 20 percent reduction of everything Penny eats.

The thyroid medication the vet prescribed for Penny raised the level of thyroid hormone in her blood and increased Penny's energy level enough for a short walk daily. The exercise helped burn more calories and encourage the muscles to get bigger and burn even more calories. As Penny lost weight and the thyroid medication did its job, the pain relievers could be given at a lower dosage, less frequently, and eventually not at all.

At home, Pat weighed herself, and then weighed herself with Penny on her scale to get a starting weight she could use at home (which might be a different number from the scale at the veterinary hospital. Penny weighed about 17.5 pounds (8 kg) at home showing a difference of 0.5 pounds (228 g). The vet told Pat that Penny's needed weight loss was an estimate, so Penny's weight on the home scale wouldn't change the estimated 4 pounds (1.8 kg) she needed to lose. Pat also could monitor weight loss by checking the fat layers on the dog's body against the BCS chart (page 140). If Penny's condition looked like a BCS of 5 after a few months, then the weight at that time would be her ideal weight.

Penny has trained Pat to reward her with a treat every time she went potty outside. When Pat started to get a biscuit from the cupboard, she remembered what her vet had said about *all* the calories in treats. The innocent act of rewarding Penny had led to significant weight gain. Instead of feeding biscuits as rewards, Pat tried

Instead of rewarding your dog with biscuits, you can try substituting veggies such as carrots. If you are going to buy treats, look for low-calorie ones made from high-quality ingredients.

lower-calorie substitutes such as the baby carrots she used for salads. Before her weight-loss regimen, Penny received five 10-calorie biscuits daily, amounting to 50 additional calories daily. Ten baby carrots, on the other hand, or one serving amount, contains just 20 calories. Penny already started the day on a good note. She was down calories and it was only morning.

Pat researched other low-calorie treats. Pat knew that Penny was sensitive to wheat gluten, so she found some all-natural, low-calorie treats that were made with real chicken, chickpeas, and no grains. Pat called the vet and asked about these low-calorie, nonallergenic treats, and the vet suggested to use a senior, limited-ingredient, low-fat kibble instead. The fat content of the diet is in the low teens, close to 10 percent. Fruit, such as pieces of apple or green beans, are good human food treat choices. Small pieces of lean meat (kibble size) are also low-calorie, and may satisfy the hunger a bit more than fruit, veggies, and treats.

After several months of sticking to daily walks, canned chicken-and-rice dog food, and cutting down on the shared food and treats, Penny slowly lost 3.5 pounds (1.6 kg) and was acting much more like her old self again. Penny was even able to walk for half an hour without too much pain. Before Penny's weight loss, Pat just thought Penny was slowing down due to her age, but she now realized that the extra weight was the real cause of the change in Penny's behavior.

At Penny's next annual exam, her BCS measured a 5 and she was down to 14 pounds (6.4 kg).

Pat and the vet consulted the resting and maintenance energy requirements chart again (see page 181) to figure out the calories for a maintenance diet given Penny's new, ideal weight. Penny's half-hour walks three to four times per week put her in the active dog category, so Pat and her vet decided to give Penny 448 calories per day, which is the calorie requirement for an active dog at about 14 pounds (5.4 kg). Penny's regular walks and thyroid medicine now allowed her to eat a bit more of the higher calorie, crunchy, grain-free dry food as long as she kept her calories at the right level. Pat

and her vet opted to feed her one-quarter crunchy or dry food, along with the canned food she currently was eating.

The vet allowed 10 percent of the daily calories to come from treats or lean, healthy human food and 25 percent from the dry food. In other words, Penny was going to get 65 percent of her calories from her canned food and 35 percent from a combination of dry food, treats, and human food. On the days Pat shared more human food, Penny wouldn't get as much dry food or treats.

For the wet food, 65 percent of her 448 calories per day comes to about 291 calories. If the canned food is 32 calories per ounce, then Penny would get about 4 ounces, or half a cup, twice daily. For the dry food, 25 percent of the 448 calories comes to 112 calories for dry food. Pat searched for a high-quality, limited-ingredient, senior, low-fat, dry dog food and found Blue Buffalo Wilderness Senior, which has 430 kcals per cup, or 53 calories per ounce, so Penny would get only 2 ounces of dry food daily. It was a surprise to Pat that dry food has more calories per ounce than canned food. That left about 45 calories for a piece of a gluten-free biscuit, veggies, or some lean meat to share.

In short, with a change in her eating habits and a daily walk, Penny's weight returned to normal (BCS of 5), and she and Pat were able to enjoy many more years together.

Keep in mind how often you offer treats to your pet and how nutritious they are. If your dog needs to lose weight, where can you cut back?

KEY POINTS

1. Consult the BCS and calorie chart on page 140 to guide you to your dog's ideal weight and the amount of calories it needs daily. Remember that both of these tools can vary widely with different dogs. Some dogs can be free fed and will have a BCS in the ideal range, other dogs will need all food measured out and accounted for.

2. Smaller pieces of treats as well as lower-calorie treats can help reduce unneeded calories. Remember that feeding extra treats is a behavioral event that both the dog owner and dog derive

pleasure from. The portion size of the treat is much less important than the event.

3. Keep your dog on the lean side to help prevent painful arthritis and undesirable medical conditions down the road. Leaner dogs have more energy, are more active, and lead better lives than their obese cousins. Counting calories and more exercise will often make a major difference. Weight loss can also decrease hip or back pain, making a dog feel years younger.

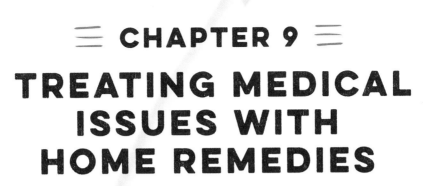

CHAPTER 9
TREATING MEDICAL ISSUES WITH HOME REMEDIES

EACH DOG MAY FACE HIS OWN SPECIFIC MEDICAL ISSUES, AND MANY OWNERS ASK WHETHER OR NOT THEIR DOG'S DIET HAS ANY EFFECT ON THESE ISSUES, IF A BETTER DIET COULD HELP CURE OR PREVENT THESE MEDICAL PROBLEMS. In this chapter, we'll explore some of the most common canine ailments and how you can take steps to improve them at home.

ITCHY SKIN AND EAR INFECTIONS

Every day in our veterinary clinic, pet owners come in with a dog that is shaking its head and scratching at its ears and skin. The causes of itchiness are varied. If a systematic approach is used to rule out the major causes, most dogs will find some relief, and some will be left with only an occasional itch.

The most common skin and ear problems are caused by the following:

Atopy: Allergies to pollens, molds, and grasses will cause itchy ears and lots of paw licking. The effects tend to be seasonal or wax and wane in intensity during the year. Benadryl without the decongestant (or any active ingredients other than diphenhydramine) may help relieve symptoms in some dogs. The dosage is 1 mg per pound twice daily.

Flea-allergy dermatitis: Flea problems and flea allergies really make a dog chew at its back legs and tail. You can tell this is the problem if you find fleas or flea poop (little black specs that turn red if placed on a wet paper towel) around the tail, head, back, and belly.

Dry, unhealthy, skin: Skin conditions can also lead to itching and infections. Adding healthy oils to the diet and using a weekly shampoo and conditioner will help moisten the skin and decrease the load of bacteria and yeast.

Food allergies: Food allergies can cause dogs to itch all over, especially at their ears and butt. If you want to find out how much of a role food sensitivity has with the red ears and itching, you need to try a very strict diet for 2 months. This is called an elimination diet or food trial.

Dogs may be sensitive to synthetic ingredients and preservatives. Some dogs will not improve until they are fed a high-quality dry diet, canned diet, prescription diet, freeze-dried raw food, raw food, or home-prepared food with natural ingredients and preservatives.

Treats that are listed as grain free and organic may still cause dogs to itch. I suggest avoiding any treats during a food trial. Use the chosen dry food or chosen meat or fish protein as a treat. Freeze-dried, raw fish or chicken make excellent grain-free treats.

FOOD TRIALS FOR ALLERGENS

You may use a food trial, also known as an elimination diet, to determine what food your dog could be reacting to. All food trials must be conducted for 2 months to get reliable results. If your dog continues to experience symptoms on the new diet, eliminate those ingredients and try a different diet to determine which foods are causing the allergies. Following are some examples of food trials, beginning with the simplest, followed by others that are more restrictive. Always use flea control in all itchy dogs to rule out a flea allergy.

1. If your dog is very mildly itchy or has dry flaky skin, feed only gluten-free biscuits and dental chews, or use gluten-free dry food as a treat. Feed your dog commercial food formulas that pair one protein with one carbohydrate such as fish/potato, duck/potato, or chicken/rice. Supplement with fish oil at 10–30 mg EPA + DHA per pound daily. Add 1 teaspoon to 1 tablespoon (5 to 15 ml) olive, canola, or coconut oil to food two to three times a week. Feed a tin of sardines twice weekly. Consider mixing in other foods such as canned, raw, or home cooked food to increase the fat percentage.

2. If your dog is mild to moderately itchy, has soft stools, or occasional diarrhea or ear infections, change to a food without beef, chicken, or gluten grains (wheat or barley). Try foods that pair a single protein and single carbohydrate such as turkey/oats or salmon/potato (beef, chicken, and wheat are considered common allergens so avoid them). Consider other types of food instead of dry food. Feed only gluten-free biscuits and dental chews, or use gluten-free dry food as a treat. Do not share steak or hamburger. Supplement with fish oil and other healthy oils, as described in diet 1. Feed one–half to two tins of sardines twice weekly.

3. If your dog is mildly to moderately itchy, has occasional ear issues, or has chronic stomach or bowel issues and you would like to try home cooking before moving on to the other choices, try recipes for home-prepared chicken/ peas/carrots, liver/eggs, or fish/potato.

(contintued)

4. If your dog is moderately itchy and has frequent ear infections or stomach and bowel issues, consider a novel-protein diet—such as fish, venison, rabbit, or kangaroo—with potato or oats. Consider canned food, dehydrated food, home-cooked food (chicken, fish, green beans, potatoes), or raw food instead of dry food. Do not serve treats or chews. Do not share any human food. Add healthy oils, bathe and condition weekly, and use ear wash twice weekly.

5. If your dog is moderately to severely itchy, and has frequent ear infections or stomach and bowel issues, change to dry or canned food that pairs a single protein and single carbohydrate such as kangaroo/lentil, venison/potato, rabbit/potato, and prescription kangaroo/oats, or a hydrolyzed diet, such as Hill's z/d or Purina HA. Avoid any commercial treats or human food. Consult a veterinary dermatologist or your vet for allergy testing. If the results are positive for environmental allergens, consider cyclosporine or other medications.

Dogs with allergies to food, fleas, or pollens may end up with a "hot spot" or red, raw, skin rash. Temporary treatment may include Benadryl, aspirin, bathing, and antibiotics along with cortisone cream. Benadryl can be used at 1 mg per pound twice daily, aspirin at 5 mg per pound twice daily. Bathe the area daily and apply creams twice daily. See your vet if the hot spot is large and painful!

EAR INFECTIONS

Many things can cause the ear canals to become inflamed or infected. Dog owners can become convinced that the dog has something stuck in there or that there are mites crawling around in the canal. The usual cause of ear infections, however, is allergies, hairy ears, small ear canals, or poor drainage.

The ear canal of the dog has an L shape. The canal heads straight down and then bends, heading toward the ear drum. While this is the optimum shape for funneling sounds to the drum, it is not so great for drainage. Small, fluffy dogs with hairy ear canals may have constant infections because that hair retains wax and moisture and prevents air from circulating. Bacteria and yeast grow easily in this warm, moist environment and produce irritating chemicals, causing itching and pain. Ear canals can also become moist from going swimming, leading to infection. Most dogs are fine after some water in the canal; they shake it out and air dry. If, however, your dog is prone to ear infections, you may want to keep it out of the water.

The most common allergies causing ear infections are environmental allergies (fleas, pollens, molds) and allergies to one or more food ingredients. Either sensitivity inflames and floods the ear canal with goo that leads to an invasion of microbes. Bacteria and yeast also produce chemicals that build up and cause discomfort. When there is a soupy, waxy buildup, the ear canals need to be cleaned and rinsed.

I advise rinsing the ears two times a week for dogs that experience chronic ear problems. If your dog's ears are a goopy mess, a few drops of Dawn detergent in warm water makes an excellent wash, followed by a diluted white vinegar rinse (vinegar to water ratio 1:10). The detergent removes the wax, and the vinegar rinse kills the bacteria and yeast. Hydrocortisone cream may also help soothe red, painful, itchy ears if applied daily. However, I don't advise ear cleaning if there are no issues. Leave healthy ears alone!

If your dog has ear problems not caused by fleas, pollen, mold, or grass allergies, and there isn't hair, small canals, excessive moisture, a tumor, or piece of something down there, then chronic ear problems may be due to food allergies. If food allergies are causing your dog's ear problems, then no amount of cleaning that will cure the condition. Ears affected by food allergies may clear for some time after medicinal treatment, but after a few weeks or months, the infection will return.

If a food allergy is the culprit, then eliminating all treats and chews and starting your dog on a limited-ingredient diet may help. Changing the diet may help many ear problems and may require several months and several food trials. Some dogs immediately improve upon switching to other ingredients, while others may take some time to figure out their ear issues. It is always worth the effort.

In order to make sure that itchy skin or ears are not caused or complicated by a medical problem, see your vet or veterinary dermatologist to rule out hypothyroidism, fleas, demodectic mange, sarcoptic mange, staph infection, ringworm, malassezia (yeast) infections, or other problems. Regularly check your dog carefully for fleas and use a really good flea control product for several months before or during a food trial. Even just a few flea bites can cause hives, redness, and hot spots.

Most health problems can be helped by adjusting nutrients in your dog's diet. For instance, diabetes can be treated with a higher-protein diet, while kidney disease requires a lower-protein diet.

BLADDER CRYSTALS AND STONES

If your dog has had problems with urinary infections and crystal formation, a moister diet (e.g., canned, raw, dehydrated, home cooked) can be helpful. They ensure higher water intake, less-concentrated urine, and fewer crystals leading to stone formation. You need to know the type of crystals or stones in order to know if a change in diet will help, and a visit to the vet is the only way to determine that. Struvite and oxalate crystals are the most common crystals that may lead to formation of urinary stones. Bladder infections and crystal formation can be tough to treat and a prescription diet, antibiotics, or surgery may be necessary to treat and prevent recurrence of the bladder crystals and stones. Struvite crystals may need only antibiotics and cranberry extract to control infection and a moister diet to dilute the urine. Dogs prone to struvite crystals may not always require a prescription diet. A grain-free, limited ingredient, moist diet may help prevent formation of struvite crystals or as they have been frequently called, triple phosphate crystals.

On the other hand, oxalate crystals and stones require a moist low-oxalate diet and potassium citrate to prevent recurrence (see recipes on page 171). You can buy a cranberry extract/potassium citrate supplement online to help prevent oxalate stones (many are combined with cranberry extract, which may help prevent bladder infections). The citrate binds to the calcium and keeps it away from the oxalate to prevent calcium oxalate crystals and stones. The citrate will also raise the pH of the urine by being metabolized to bicarbonate, which also helps prevent oxalate crystals. The twice-daily lifelong dosage is on the label.

Unfortunately, urinary stones and crystals may recur, regardless of the type of diet. Urate stones are a type of stone common to Dalmatians and occasionally seen in other breeds. Dogs experiencing these stones need a prescription diet (U/D), and if you feed a low-protein prescription diet such as U/D, I suggest adding healthy protein (an egg or a small amount of liver), as well as omega oils daily. Consult a veterinary nutritionist and use medication (allopurinol) to prevent recurrence.

Recent research suggests that probiotics at high daily dosages (5 billion CFU or more) and glucosamine/chondroitin supplements may also help prevent chronic bladder problems. I always recommend a high-quality, moist, limited-ingredient diet or prescription diet when a dog has chronic bladder issues. Make sure moist commercial diets and treats don't contain allergenic ingredients (e.g., beef, chicken, wheat gluten), which may contribute to chronic bladder inflammation. Monitor the urine for infections and crystals, by having a urinalysis done every 30 to 60 days when you are trying any type of nutritional therapy for crystal and stone prevention.

DIABETES

Diabetes can be treated with a higher-protein, higher-fiber, and lower-carbohydrate diet. If the diabetic pet is obese, a lower-fat diet is also needed. Senior diets, prescription diets, low-fat raw diets, dehydrated, and freeze-dried raw foods may help. You can also cook a meat and green veggie recipe to supplement a commercial or prescription diet; try 50 percent lean meat and organ meat with 15 percent each of green beans, peas, and carrots. Add 1 teaspoon to 1 tablespoon (5 to 15 ml) of bland Metamucil or a couple ounces of fiber cereal to the bowl with each serving. The Metamucil increases the fiber and helps control the blood sugar.

CHRONIC KIDNEY DISEASE

When the kidneys fail, a lower-protein, low-phosphorus diet is needed. A prescription diet and phosphate binder may be helpful in lowering toxic phosphate levels. If a dog's blood tests are just starting to show slightly higher levels of blood urea nitrogen (BUN) and creatinine (elements measured that reflect the kidney's filtering status) without other laboratory abnormalities, then a low-protein diet may not be absolutely necessary. The dog may need blood pressure medication, such as enalapril or amlodipine, and a high-quality moister diet with slightly lower protein (around 25 percent dry matter basis). Omega-3 fatty acids found in fish oil capsules, krill, sardines, or cod liver oil can also help (30 mg per pound of the combined omega-3 fatty acids, EPA and DHA daily).

Moist, home-cooked meals can be used to feed dogs with the beginning of kidney issues, or 10 percent home-cooked food can be mixed into the prescription kidney diet to make it tastier. You can also cook up any 50:50 meat-and-veggie mixtures for very mild chronic kidney disease, when the phosphorus levels are normal. Your vet should monitor the dog's kidney enzymes and urinalysis to know if and when a prescription diet or low phosphate diet may be needed.

CANCER

Cancer victims often need more food and better ingredients to combat their illness, but no diet I know of helps cure this awful disease. I fed my dog the best variety I could, but cancer still took Tucker, my Lab, at ten years old. Genetics plays a big part.

To help prevent cancer, avoid synthetic chemicals and preservatives in food. Only use chemical pesticides (e.g., flea, tick, heartworm control) if necessary. Consider daily omega-3 oils (30 mg per pound daily of the combined DHA and EPA portion in fish oil or other sources). Supplement with vitamin E (1–2 IU per pound of body weight daily) and use colorful veggies in the home-cooked food or make sure they are included on the label. Antioxidants, such as vitamin E, and vegetables' phytochemicals may help prevent cancer. Turmeric, an ingredient in curry, contains the phytochemical/antioxidant curcumin. Start out at 5 mg per pound and move up to 50 mg per pound daily.

If your dog has cancer, consider an excellent-quality, higher-protein, medium-fat, low-carbohydrate diet. Exercise will improve circulation, the immune system, and our furry friend's ability to fight off those nasty cells. For a great resource on the treatment of cancer, try *The Dog Cancer Survival Guide* by Dr. Demian Dressler. He also designed cancer-fighting Apocaps, a combination of ingredients including curcumin (see apocaps.com).

JOINT PAIN

Obesity and lack of exercise can lead to arthritis and sore joints. Make sure your dog has a body condition score (BCS) of a 5 out of 9 and gets some exercise at least two to three times per week. It is a

Exercise is key to treating many medical issues, including cancer and joint pain.

good idea to consider supplementing with a glucosamine/chondroitin supplement or include cartilage in the food for middle-aged dogs (over four or five years old). Raw meaty bones, slow-cooked bones, raw chicken necks, raw chicken wings, shrimp tails, and glucosamine/chondroitin/MSM supplements are all great sources of important nourishment for your dog's joints.

You can buy the joint supplements from your vet, online, or from your local pharmacy or market. Most contain 1,200 mgs of the active ingredients listed previously. At that dosage, small dogs get one-half pill daily, medium dogs get one pill daily, and large dogs get two pills daily for 6 weeks, then drop down to every other day for all dogs. I try to feed my dogs some form of cartilage two to three times a week to nourish those hardworking joints.

NAUSEA OR VOMITING

Nausea and vomiting is the most common medical symptoms I see it daily in my practice. Nauseous dogs may drool or repeatedly swallow like something is almost coming up but doesn't make it. If your dog seems really ill or is vomiting quite a bit, then you should take him into a veterinary hospital for a diagnosis and appropriate treatment. Unvaccinated young puppies that are vomiting may have a parvovirus infection and can die without supportive care. Vomiting can also be due to an inflamed pancreas. Fatty meat or a new treat may cause pancreas problems in a very sick dog, and intravenous fluids and antibiotics may be needed. Other medical problems that cause vomiting are intestinal obstruction, kidney problems, and parasites.

If the vomiting isn't severe and your dog looks pretty healthy otherwise, you can use famotidine (Pepcid AC) once daily to see if it helps. You can use one-quarter pill for a small dog, one-half pill for a medium dog, and one pill for a large dog daily.

After an episode of vomiting, it is always a good idea for the dog to fast for 12 to 24 hours or you can feed him some bland, low-fat food, such as low-fat cottage cheese and rice. Another option is chicken baby food and rice. Just use enough of the cottage cheese or baby food to flavor the bland rice. It is always better to feed small amounts several times daily.

Nauseous dogs don't need to drink lots of water. Offer ice cubes or small amounts of water several times daily. Drinking lots of water will just cause more vomiting. Pepto-Bismol may also help settle the stomach. It isn't nearly as effective as Pepcid AC but may help in really mild cases. You can give .5 to 1 teaspoon (2.5 to 5 ml) for a small dog, 1 tablespoon for a medium dog, and 1 to 2 tablespoons for a large dog two to three times daily for two or three days, in conjunction with small amounts of water or ice. These treatments are for mild cases of vomiting. Really sick dogs need a diagnosis and proper treatment.

DOCTOR'S NOTE

Vomiting can occur due to stomach irritation from eating a new food or treat, houseplant or yard plant, grass, a small piece of a toy, foil or plastic wrapping from trash, spoiled food from trash, or a dead critter.

DIARRHEA

Diarrhea is usually caused from eating something irritating, allergenic, or infectious. The same triggers listed for vomiting can also cause the runs in dogs. A change of food, a new biscuit or treat, more human food or more fat than usual, adding veggies to food, a chewed-up toy, garbage, a piece of clothing or a shoe, a plant, a dead critter, or wood or plastic from a structure can upset the stomach and bowel. Diarrhea is also caused by infections with worms, parvovirus, giardia, coccidia, bacteria, or eating raw salmon or trout guts.

Probiotics help populate the bowel with healthy bacteria and soothe an angry bowel, but the amount of helpful bacteria in yogurt may not be enough. Your local pharmacy has probiotics with 5 to 10 billion CFU of friendly bacteria per capsule. Just mix it in a small amount of baby food and rice with warm water.

Kaopectate may help coat the intestines and let the body rid itself of the bad stuff. You can give 1 to 3 tablespoons several times daily for a day or two. Try DiaGel, a product from Van Beek Natural Science, or a similar natural product, to help calm down an irritated gut. Pepto-Bismol may help soothe the bowel. Offer 0.5 to 1 teaspoon (2.5 to 5 ml) for a small dog, 1 tablespoon for a medium dog, and 1 to 2 tablespoon (7.5 to 15 ml) for a large dog two to three times daily for two or three days.

Plan to fast the dog for 12 to 24 hours, then feed only small amounts several times a day. I advise offering bland low-fat food. Low-fat cottage cheese and rice, or chicken baby food and rice, are both good options to try. Just use enough of the cottage cheese or baby food to flavor the bland rice. Once the diarrhea abates, feed smaller amounts of the regular diet two to three times a day for a couple of days.

It's always a good idea to have your pet examined or at least take a fecal sample into the vet, who can often diagnose giardia, coccidia, or worms from a sample.

COLITIS

Colitis, or blood in a formed or loose stool, can be scary for everyone. In a puppy, this could indicate parasites or parvovirus, and the pup should be checked. In an adult dog, a red spotted or swirled stool could mean an allergic reaction or intolerance to some food, biscuit, treats, or human food—or even just stress. Rarely, blood in the stool can also mean more serious things, such as a tumor, ingestions of rodent poison (causing rectal bleeding), or an anal gland abscess. Pain or illness will usually accompany a more serious situation causing bleeding, and it is always a good idea to have your dog checked out if he acts sick or appears to be in pain.

Blood in the stool can often result from feeding a new treat or a change of food; eating plants, toys, or garbage; a helping

If your dog is limping, take a look at his nails and foot pads. A broken toenail or rash may be the cause.

of fatty beef; boarding, grooming, or daycare. It may be the stress of a new dog, activity, person, or treat, but it is a very common occurrence. Always review the diet history for changes in food, treats, chews, or human food.

Dogs with red blood in the stool often act like there is nothing wrong at all, even when their stool looks like there is something really bad going on. You should always consider a trip to the vet. Even though I offer some over-the-counter (OTC) treatments, your dog may need the correct diagnostics to treat the medical condition. If you do decide to try an OTC treatment or home remedy, the following may help:

PROBIOTICS: 5 to 10 billion CFU per day will help restore the healthy balance of bacteria. They may even naturally calm the bowel and prevent future episodes. Plus, probiotics have been shown to prevent infection and even help with allergies.

KAOPECTATE: 1 to 3 tablespoons (15 to 45 ml) several times daily may help with inflammation.

BLAND DIET: White rice and chicken baby food or low-fat cottage cheese may supply nutrition without irritation.

FIBER: Sometimes fiber will help clean out the bowel. Psyllium or Metamucil is the best for that. Offer 1 teaspoon to 1 tablespoon daily for a tiny to large dog to help soothe the irritated colon. In some cases, fiber may increase the frequency or amount of diarrhea. If that happens, stop giving the fiber.

INSECT AND BEE STINGS

Insect and bee stings are common when dogs chase and eat bees and wasps. Dogs can get rewarded with a nice sting and ugly swelling on their lips and face: swelling that can make a doxie look like a shar-pei. This same swelling can occur from allergic reactions to a new food or treat. While the swelling looks dangerous and ugly, breathing problems rarely occur, unless the swelling is really severe.

If the swelling is in any way scary, proceed to the closest emergency clinic. If you would like to try an OTC medication, Benadryl (diphenhydramine), Claritin (loratadine), and Zyrtec (cetirizine) will slow the swelling. The face usually returns to normal within 12 to 48 hours. For Benadryl (25 mg, not containing decongestant), give one mg per pound two times daily. Claritin (10 mg) or Zyrtec (10 mg), give a half pill to a small dog (under 10 pounds [4.5 kg]), one pill to a medium dog (10 to 40 pounds [4.5 to 18 kg), and two pills to a large dog once or twice daily.

Large swellings that suddenly appear can also be due to an abscess from a tooth or a scratch from a dog or cat. An infected tooth will also cause a classic swelling right under or around the eye. If your swollen dog is sick due to an abscess, he may need antibiotics and treatment. If you fed a new biscuit or treat or rewarded your dog with a nice piece of steak before the swelling, consider not feeding that particular food item again.

LIMPING

Limping occurs when a dog's leg hurts, but if a dog can put weight on the leg, it is probably not broken. Most dogs like to run and play, and sometimes they overdo it. A new friend or activity may drive them to play extra hard and hurt themselves. They could sprain a joint, throw out their back, pull a muscle, or bruise something. Middle-aged dogs can hurt themselves by jumping out of the car, off the bed or sofa, or doing something they are not used to.

Dogs with these types of injuries may tremble and not move around or may yelp when they are picked up. If the injury looks severe, seek veterinary help immediately. If your furry friend doesn't look too pained, then aspirin, Benadryl, and some ice may help with swelling and pain.

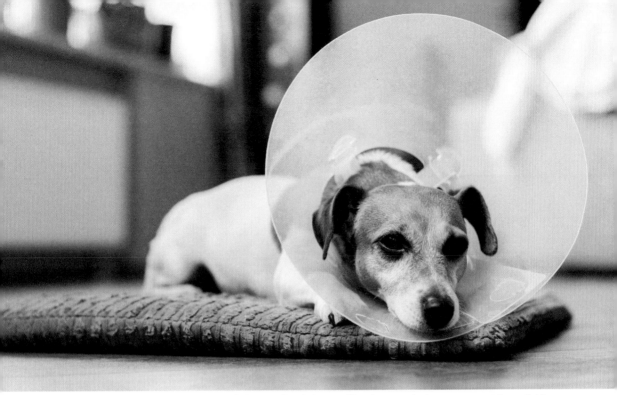

Your dog may not enjoy the "cone of shame," but it is an effective way to keep your pet from licking or chewing on cuts, stitches or other skin problems.

Take a close look at the nails and the underside of the foot for rashes, cuts, swellings, or broken toenails. Check the rest of the leg for swollen joints, bruises, infections, or cuts. Aspirin can be used for mild pain and swelling. The dose for aspirin is 5 to 10 mg per pound. One 325 mg of adult aspirin (not Tylenol or ibuprofen) per 30 pounds up to 2 tablets for a large dog or 40 to 80 mgs (one-half to one low dose aspirin) per 10 pounds (4.5 kg) twice daily can help with the discomfort and pain.

SMALL CUTS AND ABSCESSES

Small cuts and abscesses look terrible, but you can clean both with warm, soapy water, as long as your dog seems happy and not unduly bothered by the wound. If a wound is bleeding profusely or is deep, long, or painful, head to the veterinary emergency room. If the wound is small, you can use temporary first aid to see if it helps.

Dosing with aspirin (see recommendations for dosage on page 164) and applying

GIVING YOUR DOG HUMAN MEDICINE

	SYMPTOMS	SMALL DOG	MEDIUM DOG	LARGE DOG
Aspirin (325 or 80 mg pill, 5–10 mg per pound)	limping and minor injuries	½ to 1 80 mg pill 2 times daily	½ to 1 325 mg pill 2 times daily	2 325 mg pills 2 times daily
Benadryl	allergies, insect and bee stings, limping	1 mg per pound 2 times daily	1 mg per pound 2 times daily	1 mg per pound 2 times daily
Claritin (10 mg pill)	allergies, insect and bee stings	½ pill 1–2 times daily	1 pill 1–2 times daily	2 pills 1–2 times daily
Famotidine (Pepcid AC 10 mg pill)	nausea, vomiting	¼ pill daily	½ pill daily	1 pill daily
Kaopectate	diarrhea	1 tablespoon (15 g) several times daily	2 tablespoons (30 g) several times daily	3 tablespoons (45 g) several times daily
Meclizine (25 mg pill)	prevent car sickness	½ pill before driving (up to 25 pounds [11 kg])	1 pill before driving (over 25 pounds [11 kg])	1 pill before driving (over 25 pounds [11 kg])
Pepto-Bismol	nausea, diarrhea	1 tablespoon 2–3 times daily (15 g)	1 tablespoons 2–3 times daily (15 g)	1–2 tablespoons 2–3 times daily (15 to 30 g)
Probiotics	bladder issues, nausea, vomiting, diarrhea, colitis	5–10 billion CFU daily	5–10 billion CFU daily	5–10 billion CFU daily

antibiotic cream help keep discomfort and infection down until your pet can be seen by a vet. You can apply a very small amount of Krazy Glue to the edges of a small, clean, wound—without getting a bunch of glue inside—to glue a wound closed or to keep the wound in better shape for your vet.

Some stomach issues, such as diarrhea, can be eased using human medicine, such as Kaopectate and Pepto-Bismol. Consult with your veterinarian about dosage or see the chart on page 164.

To prevent your dog from chewing or licking the wound or abscess, you can put a plastic pet cone around its neck (also called a cone of shame). If you don't have one of these and the wound or bandaged area is too accessible, try covering the area with a sock or T-shirt and holding the covering in place with medical tape.

A word about wounds and bandages: First, bandages work only on the torso, paws, and lower limbs. They rarely work on the elbow or knee because they will always slip down. Second, putting one on too tight can shut off critical circulation and cause more damage. You can apply firm pressure by hand or with a bandage temporarily—just to stop the bleeding— but after a few minutes, always apply a softer pressure bandage or a sock over the injured area. Remember, if you tape the sock in place, take care not to cut off

circulation. And don't be surprised if your dog removes all your hard work in a few minutes.

SEIZURES

Seizures can look critical and very terrifying but they are dangerous only if, after one ends, the next one begins immediately, if the seizures are nonstop. Most vets won't even treat seizures with an anticonvulsant unless the seizures are frequent or severe in nature (more than one monthly). If a dog experiences severe or repeated seizures, head to the veterinary emergency hospital.

If your dog comes out of the seizure in a few minutes and looks a little groggy, but otherwise no worse for wear, you could probably delay a trip to the vet until the

To remove a tick, pinch it as close to the skin as you can and pull it off. If the bite looks infected, antibiotic ointment may be in order.

TICKS

Ticks jump on pets and attach themselves to the skin a short time after contact. To remove them, pinch the tick as close to the skin as you can and slowly pull until the tick comes off. Use gloves so as not to come in direct contact with the tick; it contains bacteria and could cause illness. After you remove the tick, wash your hands thoroughly.

There is often a residual bump and redness at the tick-bite site for several weeks. That is the result of bite penetration, saliva, body parts, and infectious bacteria. If the bite does not look too swollen or infected, antibiotic ointment will help with any minor infection, and cortisone cream can relieve swelling. And yes, it's safe for your dog to lick the treated area. Ask your vet if your dog should get antibiotics or be tested for Lyme disease or other tick-borne diseases.

next day. Your vet will rule out the other causes of the seizures other than epilepsy with an exam, blood work, or x-rays. Just as with diarrhea and vomiting, seizures can occur after feeding a piece of steak or gluten containing biscuit or chews.

Did you know an ice pack could help? An ice pack applied to the back from the middle of the thoracic vertebrae to the middle of the lumbar vertebrae has been found to decrease the severity and length of seizures, if applied immediately.

My dog, Maisy, is prone to petit mal seizures and may experience them after eating a piece of beef. Studies show that meat-based protein sources trigger a more severe response compared to vegetable and dairy proteins. In our practice, I have found that avoiding beef and feeding a grain-free diet has decreased the frequency and severity of seizures.

BROKEN TOENAILS

Broken toenails are painful and often lead to limping. When a dog's toenails do not wear down naturally, they become long and can get caught or bent until they break. Broken nails can be quite painful and annoying, but they're generally not critical. You can use aspirin, antibiotic cream, and a bandage or sock as a temporary fix. If the nail is completely ripped off, you may even apply a Soft Paw (softpaws.com) over the bloody quick (the tender part inside a dog's nail that contains nerves and blood vessels). In severe cases, your vet may need to sedate your dog and remove the pieces of nail still embedded in the toe.

CAR SICKNESS

Car sickness or motion sickness is common until a dog becomes used to the ride and used to seeing things pass by so quickly. Some of us went through the same thing as children and needed pharmaceutical assistance. Offer meclizine (25 mgs) 30 minutes to 1 hour before travel—half a pill to dogs under 25 pounds (11.3 kg) and a whole pill to dogs over 25 pounds (11.3 kg). Don't use meclizine (brand name Dramamine), on dogs with medical problems or that are pregnant.

KEY POINTS

DOCTOR'S NOTE

If your dog needs help, head to the veterinary ER! This chapter is not a substitute for veterinary diagnosis and treatment. It is meant to be helpful only in mild medical conditions. Seek help if your dog is sick or in pain!

1. Keep OTC medications on hand for minor ailments. If giving the proper dosage, dogs can get relief from minor pains and sicknesses by taking human medicines such as aspirin, Benadryl, and Pepcid AC.

2. Avoid known allergens in foods, treats, biscuits, or dental chews. If your dog is itchy and inflamed, avoid allergenic ingredients or feed a limited-ingredient diet. Beef, chicken, wheat, dairy, and soy food, treat, or chew ingredients may cause vomiting, diarrhea, itchy skin, red ears, bladder problems, or even seizures in sensitive dogs.

3. The more moisture and fewer synthetic additives in food, the better!

Canned, raw, semimoist, home-cooked, or rehydrated food may really help sensitive dogs deal with skin, ear, stomach, bladder, and bowel issues. Moister food and less allergens seem to help most dogs feel and look better. Don't forget the probiotics, which can improve overall digestion and even prevent allergies and infection!

APPENDIX A
RECIPES

I first started cooking for my pets as a way to introduce healthful ingredients and to help clients who had dogs with health problems. I wanted to find a more economical dog food for clients that could not afford more expensive canned, dehydrated, raw, or prescription diets. After cooking for my pack of three and seeing the positive effects home-cooked food had on my own dogs, I became their full-time cook.

Cooking food in a slow cooker is much easier than most other ways of preparing dog food. Combining the ingredients and starting the pot takes only minutes, and it's appealing to those people who shy away from home cooking because they think it takes too much time.

I started by using ingredients listed on the ingredient label of products such as canned food. Instead of adding mineral supplements, I leave the slow-cooked softened, crumbly bones in the stew. (You sometimes have to stir through the stew to break up bones or remove the middle of the long bones.) Bones may take up to 16 hours to soften.

Slow-cooked dog food may have more fat and vegetables than most canned foods, and may cause stomach or bowel upset in some dogs. If your pets do not have major medical problems and have tolerated food changes in the past, you can start the transition to home-cooked food by slow cooking or cooking on the stove a small batch of food. Add increasing amounts to their normal diet and watch for vomiting, indigestion, or gas. Those are signs that their digestive tract either needs some time to adjust to them, which can take days or even weeks, or doesn't like the ingredients if the symptoms persist. Other signs of allergic reactions to food are hives, itchiness, or red, itchy ears. If your dog seems happy and has normal stools, then increase the amount of home-cooked food. The usual amount to add is 25 percent each day to arrive at 100 percent over four days (25/50/75/100).

To save time, cook a large batch and portion out your estimate for the amount of food your dog or dogs would eat in 1 week. Keep the week's supply in the refrigerator and freeze the rest in resealable freezer bags or other suitable containers. Thaw before feeding, but after that do not leave the food out for longer than meal time or allow it to warm up!

Be careful with home cooking if your dog has had problems with pancreatitis. Dogs that have had pancreas issues need to eat a low-fat, limited-ingredient diet. They also should be transitioned very carefully over a longer period of time—7 to 10 days. That means 10 to 15 percent home-cooked food should be added to their normal diet each day. If you feed your dog 8 ounces of total food, for example, then each day you would feed 1 ounce less of the old food and 1 ounce more of the new food every day.

I recommend starting with chicken unless your dog has a known intolerance to chicken. If your dog can't eat chicken, use the Limited-Ingredient Diet on page 170.

LOW-FAT STARTER RECIPE

For the first batch of slow-cooked dog food, I recommend making a small amount and using low-fat meat or fish combined with white or brown rice.

1 pound (454 g) cubed, skinless, boneless chicken breast, or lean beef, turkey, or fish

1 to 3 ounces (85 g) chicken liver, hearts, and gizzards

2 whole eggs (including shells)

1 teaspoon (1,500 mg) bonemeal (per pound of meat)

4 ounces (113 g) uncooked white rice

1 can (14.5 oz. or 411 g) green beans

Water

In a slow cooker, combine the chicken breasts, chicken liver, chicken hearts, gizzards, and eggs. Add 1 teaspoon (1,750 mg) of bonemeal per pound of meat. Add the white rice and green beans. Add water to cover the ingredients, and then stir to mix in the eggs. Cook on low for 4 to 8 hours until the breasts fall apart. Stir and add water if needed to make a moister stew. Let the mixture cool and refrigerate.

Yeild: 7–8 cups (60 oz)

HIGHER-FAT RECIPE

After a week on a low-fat recipe, or if you know your dog will tolerate a higher fat recipe, you can try the following ingredients:

4-pound (1.8 kg) whole young fryer, skin removed

4 ounces (113 g) chicken livers

4 ounces (113 g) chicken hearts and gizzards

2 pounds (908 g) frozen green beans

4 eggs

Water

8 ounces (227 g) uncooked brown rice

Put the chicken, organs, green beans, and eggs in a slow cooker. Add enough water to cover. Cook on high for 12 to 18 hours. Check after several hours of cooking and add water, if needed.

After 12 hours, when meat is falling off soft bones, stir in the uncooked brown rice. After 14 to 18 hours (could be more in some cookers), when bones crumble easily, stir well, turn off the slow cooker, and let cool. Remove the middle of long bones, if hard. Break off and leave in the joints—they are good joint nutrition for your dog!

Yeild: 16–18 cups (135 oz)

IMPORTANT SUPPLEMENTS

If you don't include the softened bones or feed raw bones, you'll need to supplement the home-cooked food with bonemeal. Add the amount of bonemeal equal to 1,500 mg of calcium per pound of meat (1 teaspoon bonemeal per pound of meat.) Supplement with vitamin E at 1 IU per pound of dog daily, or larger doses can be given twice weekly.

I also encourage feeding sardines twice weekly (1 to 2 tins) or fish-oil capsules at one 1,000 mg capsule per 10 to 30 pounds (4.5 to 13.5 kg) daily. The lower range is for healthy dogs and the higher range is for dogs with any skin, heart, kidney, joint, immune, or other medical issues. A typical capsule has 300 mg of the active combined omega-3 fatty acids, DHA, and EPA.

If you don't add liver to your home-cooked food, supplement with .5 to 1 teaspoon (2.5 to 5 ml) of cod liver oil daily and at least 1000 IU of vitamin A daily.

Recipe Note: If your dog is allergic to chicken, you'll want to test your dog's tolerance for other meats, as well. Feed a small, cooked low-fat piece of meat such as fish, turkey, pork loin, or ground hamburger for a few days and watch for any skin or ear allergies or bowel reactions. Also avoid the meats or fish your dog does not tolerate in commercial food, treats, or chews.

LIMITED-INGREDIENT DIET

A limited-ingredient diet starts out with one source of protein and fat, combined with one carbohydrate such as sweet potatoes or rice. After 2 months of feeding this diet, you can slowly add other meat or veggies to the mix, watching for any skin, ear, or bowel problems.

Be sure to use a low-fat protein—chicken (skinless thighs, mostly skinless fryer, breasts with skins), lean turkey, pork, beef, fish, or eggs—that your dog can tolerate (and that he enjoys!). To test for allergies, follow the instructions in the Recipe Note on page 169 or see Food Trials on page 150.

Hundreds of people have home-cooked these types of recipes, but they are not analyzed for vitamin and mineral content. Depending on the ingredients used, supplements added, or shared healthy foods, these home-prepared diets may not be complete and balanced. The Honest Kitchen has a dehydrated base that is nutritionally complete and balanced to which you can add the meat. Balance IT offers a veterinary nutritional service to balance home-prepared dog food (https://secure.balanceit.com/). You can also seek advice from a veterinary nutritionist.

HOME-PREPARED, LIMITED INGREDIENT DIET

Home-prepared, limited-ingredient diets may need to be supplemented with bonemeal, vitamin E and cod liver oil, and may need other vitamins, depending if bones or organs are used in the mix.

2 to 3 (907 to 1,360 g) pounds low-fat meat, eggs, or fish (choose one protein source)

4 ounces (113 g, weight will vary) chicken, beef, pork, or venison liver 4 ounces (170 g, weight will vary) chicken or beef hearts

4 to 6 cups water

2 pounds (907 g) sweet potatoes or 8 ounces (226 g) uncooked white rice

Bonemeal (1 teaspoon per pound of meat unless bones are included or raw meaty bones are fed)

Place the meat in a slow cooker. Add the liver, heart, and potatoes (if using). Cover the mixture with water. Cook for 4 to 6 hours until stewlike. (Cook 12 to 18 hours if chicken bones are included). Don't add bonemeal if chicken bones are included.

After a few hours, add more water to desired consistency. If not using potatoes, add rice and stir. Let cook for 1 hour, then cool and refrigerate.

Always supplement with sardines, fish or krill oil capsules or liquid several times weekly. If liver is not used, supplement with 0.5 to 1 teaspoon cod liver oil daily. Supplement with vitamin E (1 IU per pound daily).

Yeild: 12–14 cups (75 oz)

LOW-OXALATE DIET

This diet may help prevent oxalate crystals and stones in dogs prone to forming them by reducing the amount of oxalates in the food. Citrate as potassium citrate (30 mg per pound of dog's weight twice daily) or calcium citrate (500 mg per pound of food) should also be added to bind up the excess calcium in the urinary system to prevent binding with the oxalates present. The ratio is 50 percent poultry and eggs, meat, and fish; 25 percent peas and fruit; and 25 percent rice or potatoes. Add 1 teaspoon of bone meal per pound of meat.

Chicken breasts with skin or skinned fryer

Lean turkey, beef, or fish

Eggs

Peas

Banana

White rice or skinless red potatoes

Bonemeal

Combine all of the ingredients in a slow cooker. Cover the ingredients with water and cook for 4 to 5 hours on high. Stir and add water if needed to make a moister stew. Let the mixture cool and refrigerate.

Supplement this recipe with 0.5 to 1 teaspoon cod liver oil; 2 IU vitamin E per pound of dog's weight; cranberry/potassium citrate (pills or powder) daily.

Check out the detailed low-oxalate diet at http://dogaware.com/articles/wdjcalciumoxalates.html#recipe.

Yield: 18 cups (135 oz)

EASY EGGS AND RICE

This is a really easy, economical, and high-quality protein recipe.

24 eggs

8 ounces (227 g) uncooked brown rice, or 24 ounces (680 g) diced sweet potatoes

2 pounds (907 g) frozen peas and carrots

2 teaspoons bone meal (or 2,600 mg)

6 cups water

Add all the ingredients to a slow cooker and cook for 4 hours. Stir well to blend ingredients, adding water as needed.

Supplement this recipe with 0.5 to 1 teaspoon cod liver oil daily, and vitamin E supplement (1 IU per pound of dog's weight) daily.

Yield: 18 cups (135 oz)

You can use these basic recipes to combine low-fat meat, fish, eggs, organs, vegetables, and nongluten grains. I like the idea of feeding different combinations of meats, veggies, and rice to try and cover all the nutritional bases.

In addition to chicken, some clients hunt or fish and feed elk, venison, catfish, or other fish or game to their dogs. Colorful vegetables and fruit contain vital antioxidants and phytochemicals to fight inflammation and cancer. Start with two or three ingredients, and slowly transition so your dog can get used to the new amount of fat and vegetables in the diet.

Most home-cooked diets prepared with lean meat have about 25 to 35 calories per ounce. An 8-ounce (226 g) serving of chicken and vegetable stew would have about 250 calories. You can use the BCS, score, and calorie count from the chart, or feed the same amount of home-cooked food as canned food. Always monitor the weight when you are making changes to the diet. Many clients have raved about the effects of a home-cooked diet on their dog's health. With home cooking, you can use the best ingredients available to you and mix them the way that is best for your dog's health.

Here's a list of common ingredients and proportions I use:

Meat and organs (50 percent of the total weight of the mix): chicken, salmon, tilapia, ground turkey, pork loin, low-fat hamburger, bison, venison, lamb, salmon, salmon head, liver (1 ounce per pound of meat), hearts and gizzards (1 to 2 ounces per pound of meat), beef heart, beef liver, venison liver, pork liver

Carbohydrates (50 percent of the total weight of the mix): sweet potatoes, white potatoes, brown rice, oats, white rice, green beans, peas and carrots, tomatoes, squash, broccoli, cauliflower, garbanzo beans, kidney beans, lentils, pumpkin, eggplant, kale, spinach, apples, berries, and bananas.

APPENDIX B
INGREDIENT GLOSSARY

Blue Buffalo, one of the most popular commercial dog food companies, provides a fantastic glossary of ingredients, that defines all the ingredients we discuss in this book and will help you decipher food labels. Following is a version of that glossary, specially adapted for this book. You can find the original at bluebuffalo.com/ingredients. (Throughout this glossary *BLUE* refers to Blue Buffalo's products. Reprinted with permission.)

A

Alfalfa is one of the richest mineral foods containing abundant amounts of trace minerals (zinc, iron, and manganese), vitamins (vitamin A, vitamin C).

Apples are an excellent source of pectin, a water-soluble fiber.

Arginine is an amino acid that promotes growth, muscle building, and healing as well as fat burning. Known to be an immune booster and cancer fighter.

B

Bacillus Lactobacillus Acidophilus, Bacillus Subtilis, Bifidobacterium Thermophilum, Bifidobacterium Longum, and *Enterococcus Faecium* are active dehydrated cultures added to *BLUE* dog and cat foods after processing. They are activated upon ingesting the food and help to maintain a normal bacterial balance in the lower intestine. They aid in digestion and reduce the occurrence of diarrhea, contributing to colon and rectum health.

Bacon is a cut of meat taken from a pig that has been cured, smoked, or both, often used for flavor.

Whole Barley is the whole grain with the hull and bran. It is a good carbohydrate source for energy, B vitamins, and fiber for colon health. It is an excellent source of soluble fiber and has been shown to lower cholesterol levels. Barley is a quality grain source but still may cause medical issues if a dog is sensitive to gluten grains.

Barley Grass is a good source of chlorophyll, fiber, and phytochemicals. It has been known to be beneficial in the treatment of arthritis, diabetes, kidney and liver disease, and cancer.

Beef is a great source of protein, vitamin B12, selenium, zinc, iron, and other B vitamins (can be allergenic in sensitive dogs).

Beta-Carotene plays an important role in animal health as a precursor of vitamin A, which is an essential nutrient needed for normal growth development, reproduction, immune function, and vision. It also acts as an antioxidant and a potent quencher of singlet oxygen. Singlet oxygen and free radicals are unstable chemicals that can arise from normal body metabolism or from environmental exposure to cigarette smoke, air pollutants, radiation, certain drugs, and environmental toxins. If not neutralized, they can cause serious cellular damage leading to certain chronic diseases.

Biotin is active in the metabolism of fats, carbohydrates, protein, and the formation of fatty acids. It promotes normal health of sweat glands, nerve tissue, bone marrow, blood cells, skin, and hair. It is essential for growth and well-being.

Blackberries are low-calorie, high-fiber berries packed with folate, vitamins, minerals, and antioxidants.

Blueberries are an excellent source of vitamins A and C, potassium, and fiber.

Broccoli is rich in vitamins A and C and calcium and is an excellent source of antioxidants.

Brown Rice is a natural, whole grain rice that is associated with natural health foods. The bran portion provides essential B vitamins, minerals, and fiber. Brown rice is an excellent, high-quality complex carbohydrate source for energy and fiber for colon health.

C

Calcium is vital for the formation of strong bones and teeth. It also promotes healthy muscle and tissue growth. (Calcium needs to be added to balance the phosphorus present in meat. The ratio of calcium to phosphorus should range from 1:1 to 2:1. In large-breed growing puppies, a slightly lower amount of calcium and phosphorus is used in large breed puppy food. Home-cooked food should always contain added calcium.)

Calcium Carbonate is a mineral compound that is commonly used as a calcium supplement.

Calcium Iodate is a source of calcium and iodine.

Calcium Pantothenate (Vitamin B5) is one of the B vitamins; it acts as a coenzyme in the conversion of amino acids and is important for healthy skin. It also promotes normal growth and development and aids in the release of energy from foods.

Calcium Phosphate is another source of calcium.

Canola Oil is obtained by extracting the oil from canola seeds, providing calories for energy and omega-3 and -6 fatty acids for a healthy coat.

Carrageenan Gum is a natural ingredient derived from red kelp and used as a thickener and stabilizer in canned food. It may irritate the gut in sensitive dogs.

Carrots provide antioxidants and health-protecting phytochemicals, vitamins, and minerals. They are high in vitamin A and carotenoids. Carotenoids are antioxidants providing protection against free radicals (cancer-causing agents). The carrots used in *BLUE* dog and cat foods are whole, fresh carrots sourced from USDA-approved sources.

Cellulose is the organic plant material found in fruits, vegetables, and some grains that acts as a stool softener.

Chelated Minerals are minerals that get into the bloodstream more readily. *BLUE* uses minerals that are chelated or "attached to" easily absorbable amino acids. As a result, *BLUE* minerals are up to four times more readily absorbed than commonly used inorganic minerals.

Chicken is a high-quality, highly digestible protein source that provides essential amino acids, fatty acids, and certain minerals for muscle development, organ function, and energy. The chicken used in *BLUE* natural dog and cat foods comes from USDA-inspected facilities.

Chicken Fat is a high-quality source of essential fatty acids and energy. It is also high in linoleic acid (source of omega-6 fatty acids), which helps promote healthy skin and coat. The chicken fat in *BLUE* natural dog and cat foods comes from USDA-inspected facilities and is stabilized with natural, mixed tocopherols and rosemary to maintain freshness.

Chicken Liver is an organ meat high in protein, rich in iron and vitamin A, and used as a natural flavor enhancer.

Chicken Meal is a highly digestible protein source produced by cooking chicken at high temperatures, extracting the fat, and drying the meat residue. It is a meat protein, providing essential amino and fatty acids, vitamins, and minerals for muscle development and energy. It is naturally stabilized with mixed tocopherols and rosemary to preserve freshness.

Chicory Root is a perennial Old World herb cultivated as a source of inulin, known as a prebiotic, that feeds the good bacteria and hinders the growth of bad bacteria in pets' digestive tract.

Choline Chloride protects nerve function and maintains fat metabolism. It also helps regulate the liver and helps maintain acid and water balance.

Chondroitin Sulfate is a naturally occurring compound believed to be helpful in the maintenance and rebuilding of joint cartilage.

Cinnamon is from the aromatic bark of certain tropical trees that is dried and ground for use as a spice; it contains calcium, iron, vitamins C and K, and manganese.

Copper promotes normal red blood cell formation, acts as a catalyst in the storage and release of iron to form hemoglobin for red blood cells, assists in the production of several enzymes involved in respiration, promotes connective-tissue formation and central nervous system function, and promotes normal insulin function. Copper is an essential mineral for preventing anemia in dogs and cats.

Cranberries are an antioxidant that fights free radicals (toxins) in the body; it is a natural acidifier that contributes to urinary tract health, preventing bacterial infection in the urinary tract, and aids in the prevention of struvite crystals in the bladder and urethra.

D

Dicalcium Phosphate is a mineral compound that is used as a nutritional source of calcium and phosphorus to help with bone health.

Dried *Lactobacillus Acidophilus, Enterococcus Faecium,* and *Bacillus Subtilis Fermentation Products* have *Lactobacillus acidophilus, Bacillus subtilis, Bifidobacterium thermophilum, Bifidobacterium longum,* and *Enterococcus faecium*, which are active dehydrated cultures added to *BLUE* dog and cat foods after processing. They are activated when ingested and help maintain normal bacterial balance in the lower intestine. They aid in digestion and reduce the occurrence of diarrhea, contributing to colon and rectum health.

Dried Yeast has *Saccharomyces cerevisiae*, another probiotic for intestinal health.

E

Eggs are a source of high-quality protein and fatty acids. It is a complete protein source providing all the essential amino acids for growth and muscle development. The fatty acid profile includes arachidonic acid and omega-6 fatty acids associated with healthy skin and coat. The eggs used in *BLUE* products are whole and fresh from USDA-approved facilities.

F

Fish Meal is an excellent source of protein and omega fatty acids that help the skin and coat, growth, and development.

Flaxseeds contains flaxseed oil, which is one of the richest sources of the essential omega-3 fatty acids (linolenic acid). Flax is a good source of essential amino acids and contains all the essential vitamins and minerals required by dogs and cats. It is beneficial for its anti-inflammatory effect and has been known to help arthritis and prevent cancer. Flaxseed is also a great fiber source that aids in digestion and an excellent source of omega-3 and omega-6 fatty acids that promote healthy skin and coat.

Folic Acid is a water-soluble B vitamin that plays an important role in various cellular functions.

G

Garlic is a natural antioxidant that can help thin the blood, helps strengthen the heart and maintain good circulation, and has natural antibiotic properties from allicin. Large amounts could cause anemia in sensitive dogs.

Ginger promotes digestive health, stimulates the immune system, and is known to help with arthritis.

Glucosamine prevents arthritis and helps to maintain connective tissue, tendons, ligaments, and cartilage.

Ground Millet is a nutritious grain that is high in fiber, which helps with digestion, and B-complex vitamins, which support cellular function.

Guar Gum is primarily used as a thickener and stabilizer in canned food. It is a highly soluble and highly digestible fiber with a low caloric content and is known to significantly reduce cholesterol levels.

H

Herring Oil is a source of omega-3 fatty acids.

I

Iron Amino Acid Chelate is an essential mineral for preventing anemia and stimulating bone-marrow production of hemoglobin. Hemoglobin is the red-blood-cell pigment that carries oxygen to body cells and forms part of several enzymes and proteins.

K

Kelp is a good source of essential vitamins and minerals (including iodine). It is also a good antioxidant and has been known to be beneficial in helping to protect against cancer.

L

Lamb is a highly digestible protein source providing essential amino acids, fatty acids, vitamins, and minerals for muscle development, energy, and coat condition. Amino acids and fatty acids are more readily available in lamb because it is not subjected to a high-heat process. Lamb used in *BLUE* pet foods is New Zealand free-range lamb and is hormone, antibiotic, and steroid free.

Lamb Meal is a highly digestible protein source produced by cooking lamb at high temperatures, extracting the fat, and drying the meat residue. It is a meat protein, providing essential amino acids and fatty acids, vitamins, and minerals for muscle development and energy. It is naturally stabilized with mixed tocopherols and rosemary to preserve freshness.

L-Carnitine is an amino acid that increases fat metabolism, lowers cholesterol and triglyceride levels. It also promotes enhanced endurance.

Lentils are rich in B vitamins and protein. It is also rich in fiber, which promotes a healthy heart and lower cholesterol.

L-Lysine is needed for proper growth and bone development. It aids in the production of antibodies, hormones, and enzymes as well as collagen formation and tissue repair.

M

Manganese Amino Acid Chelate contains manganese, an essential mineral for normal growth and development, aids in carbohydrate metabolism, promotes nerve functions, aids in the formation of connective tissue and is involved in the antioxidation process.

Menhaden Fish Meal is a meal obtained from processing fish of the menhaden species. It is an excellent source of high-quality fish protein and omega-3 essential fatty acids including EPA (eicosapentaenoic acid), DHA (docosahexaenoic acid), and arachionic acid.

N

Natural Chicken Flavor is a liquefied or dried chicken tissue that is used as a flavor enhancer.

Natural Flavors are parts of processed fruits, vegetables, spices, or fermentation products that are used for flavoring.

Niacin (vitamin B3) is also called nicotinic acid or nicotinamide. It is essential for healthy nerves and skin. It is important in the metabolism of carbohydrates, proteins, and fats; reduces cholesterol and triglycerides in the blood; and is key for the proper health of the central nervous and GI systems.

O

Oat Fiber is the outer casing of the oat grain that helps move food through the digestive tract slowly, which helps to optimize the absorption of nutrients; it also helps to lower cholesterol. (It promotes the good balance of bacteria in the colon and is a nongluten grain.)

Oat Flour is ground, whole oats, which are an excellent source of highly digestible carbohydrates, protein, and nutritional fibers.

Oatmeal is an excellent carbohydrate source for energy. It is a high-quality grain source that is rich in B vitamins and minimizes allergic reactions typically associated with wheat and corn. It may help in controlling blood sugar.

Omega-3 and -6 are fatty acids associated with improved immune response and are potential anti-inflammatory aids and important for kidney, heart, brain, skin, and joint health. Fats are also the energy source for the body.

P

Pantothenic Acid is needed for the metabolism of fats and fatty acids and the production of hormones, sterols, and enzymes. It is helpful in the prevention of diseases of the GI tract and the immune system, particularly diseases of the adrenal gland system. It is also important in cell building and the central nervous system.

Parsley is an herb associated with reducing urinary tract inflammation: It aids in digestion and increases renal function to help the body dispose of excessive fluid by increasing urine production. It also contains vitamins A and C, which are associated with antioxidant properties.

Peas are a good source of protein and vitamin A. They are packed with fiber to help manage cholesterol and blood sugar, and they are a good source of potassium. *BLUE* uses fresh, green peas.

Pomegranate is a naturally powerful antioxidant

Potassium is important for a healthy nervous system and a regular heart rhythm. It aids in proper muscle contraction and maintaining stable blood pressure.

Potassium Iodide is used as a bioavailable source of iodide. Iodide is essential for thyroid health, promotes normal cell function, and is important in the formation of bones, teeth, muscles, and blood.

Potatoes provide B vitamins, carbohydrates, vitamin C, potassium, iron and magnesium. *BLUE* uses whole, fresh potatoes.

Potato Starch is a good source of fiber.

Psyllium is an excellent soluble fiber source that helps with digestion.

Pumpkins are a great source of flavor and fiber; are packed with vitamins, minerals, and antioxidants; and help promote healthy digestion.

Pyridoxine Hydrochloride (Vitamin B$_6$) is essential for the metabolism of proteins. It acts as a cofactor for the large hydrochloride number of enzymes involved in amino acid and metabolism. It is also involved in the metabolism of the precursor of heme, a compound of blood that helps in the normal function of the brain.

R

Riboflavin (Vitamin B$_2$) is important for digestion of fats and carbohydrates; healthy skin and coat, and normal growth and development.

Rice Bran is the outer husk and germ of the rice grain. It is a good fiber source as well as one of the richest sources of vitamins, minerals, and antioxidants.

Rosemary and Rosemary Extract are excellent natural preservatives that are also know to help protect against cancer.

Rye is a grain that provides high-quality carbohydrates for energy. It is not commonly used in pet foods and may cause issues in animals sensitive to gluten grains.

Salmon is an excellent source of protein and omega fatty acids that help skin and coat, growth, and development.

Salmon Meal is a highly digestible protein source produced by cooking salmon at high temperatures, extracting the fat, and drying the remaining meat. Because it is a meat protein, salmon meal provides essential amino acids, omega-3 fatty acids, vitamins, and minerals for muscle development and energy.

Salmon Oil is high in omega-3 fatty acid.

Salt is a supplement for sodium and chloride, essential electrolytes required by dogs and cats. They help regulate water balance in the body, aid in muscle contraction and nerve transmission, and regulate the body's acid balance

Sea Salt is a natural form of salt obtained from processing seawater. Sea salt also contains trace minerals needed for animal health.

Sodium Selenite is a source of selenium. Selenium is important to healthy muscles and nerves. It is also important in fertility and enhances the antioxidant characteristics of vitamin E.

Spinach is an excellent source of fiber, phytonutrients, omega-3 fatty acids, vitamins, and minerals. It is naturally packed with antioxidants and has many health benefits.

Spirulina is a blue-green algae that grows on the surface of alkaline lakes. It is one of the oldest plants on the planet. Algae are associated with providing therapeutic as well as nutritional value. Spirulina contains B-complex vitamins, beta-carotene, gamma-linolenic acid, iron, and protein. Health benefits have been associated with improving immunity and increasing beneficial bacteria in the intestine for colon-tract health.

Sunflower Oil has is obtained from processing sunflower seeds. It is an excellent source of omega-6 fatty acids also containing 62 to 70 percent linoleic acid. Omega-6 fatty acids are associated with coat and skin health. Sunflower oil used in *BLUE* dog and cat foods is naturally stabilized with natural mixed tocopherols (a source of vitamin E) to provide freshness.

Sweet Potatoes are an excellent source of potassium, B vitamins, and beta-carotene. They provide phytochemicals and carotenoids, sources of antioxidant agents providing natural protection against free radicals (cancer-causing agents). The sweet potatoes used in BLUE dog and cat foods are fresh, whole sweet potatoes sourced from USDA-approved vendors.

T

Thiamine Mononitrate (Vitamin B$_1$) is essential for the metabolism of carbohydrates and protein. It is also important for a healthy nervous system, keeps mucous membranes healthy, and maintains normal function of the nervous system, muscles, and heart. It also promotes normal growth and development.

Tocopherols are an excellent source of vitamin E, a powerful antioxidant that protects against cell damage from free radicals (cancer-causing agents). It also helps maintain normal heart and joint function.

Tomato Pomace is a mixture of tomato skins, pulp, and crushed seeds. It is an excellent source of soluble fiber and is rich in the antioxidant lycopene.

Tuna is an excellent source of protein and omega fatty acids that help skin and coat and aid in growth and the development of the nervous system.

Turkey is an excellent source of protein and is rich in calcium, potassium, B vitamins, niacin, iron, and zinc, which promote energy and overall health. It is low in cholesterol and easy to digest.

Turkey Meal is dry, rendered, or cooked ground turkey that is a high-quality protein source.

Turmeric is an herb associated with aiding digestion by helping to stimulate the flow of bile, which helps digest fat.

V

Vitamin A is essential for healthy bones, teeth, hair, skin, eyes, and mucous membranes. It is an oil-soluble vitamin and is important to the immune system especially for respiratory infections. It is a building block of rhodopsin, a compound in the retina responsible for sight in partial darkness.

Vitamin B12 is a coenzyme in nucleic acid, protein, and lipid synthesis. It is necessary for growth and for normal processing of carbohydrates, protein, and fat in the body.

Vitamin C is a potent antioxidant and immune booster. It helps to keep teeth and bones strong.

Vitamin D promotes healthy skin, bones, connective tissue, and heart. It is necessary for the proper absorption and utilization of calcium and phosphorus.

Vitamin E is a potent antioxidant that helps prevent free radicals and inflammation that harm organs and cause cancer.

W

Whitefish in commercial food typically consists of nonrendered, deboned, clean whitefish meat. It is an excellent source of protein, as well as niacin, phosphorus, and selenium. It is also low in sodium.

Y

Yellow Squash is rich in vitamins A and C and calcium.

Yellow Zucchini is very low in calories and a good source of vitamin C and manganese.

Yucca Schidigera Extract is a natural extract made entirely from the stem of the Yucca Schidigera plant. It supports anti-inflammatory processes in tendons and joint cartilage.

Z

Zinc (and Zinc Amino Acid Chelate) is an essential mineral important in helping to support healthy skin, hair, and mucous membranes. It has antioxidant properties, helps maintain normal senses of taste and smell, aids in healing and promoting a healthy immune system, helps synthesize DNA and RNA, and promotes normal growth and development.

APPENDIX C
DAILY CALORIES CHART

LBs	KGs	RER*/wt. loss	Puppy (1–4mo)	Puppy (4–6mo)	Adult (2–8 years) (Inactive)	Adult (Active)	Senior (8 years + older) (Inactive)	Senior (Active)
2	0.9	63	189	126	82	101	76	95
4	1.8	105	315	210	136	168	126	158
6	2.7	147	441	294	191	235	176	221
8	3.6	182	546	364	237	291	218	273
10	4.5	217	651	434	282	347	260	326
12	5.5	252	756	504	328	403	302	378
14	6.4	280	840	560	364	448	336	420
16	7.3	308	924	616	400	493	370	462
18	8.2	336	1008	672	437	538	403	504
20	9	364	1092	728	473	582	437	546
25	11.4	434	1329	868	564	694	521	651
30	13.6	497	1491	994	664	795	596	746
35	15.9	560	1680	1120	728	896	672	840
40	18.2	616	1848	1232	801	986	739	924

*Resting Energy Requirements

LBs	KGs	RER /wt. loss	Puppy (1-4mo)	Puppy (4-6mo)	Adult (Inactive)	Adult (Active)	Senior (Inactive)	Senior (Active)
45	20.5	672	2016	1344	873	1075	806	1008
50	22.7	728	2184	1456	946	1165	874	1092
55	25	784	2352	1568	1019	1254	941	1176
60	27.3	833	2499	1666	1083	1254	1000	1250
65	29.5	889	2667	1778	1156	1422	1067	1334
70	31.8	938	2814	1876	1219	1501	1126	1407
75	34.1	987	2961	1972	1283	1579	1184	1481
80	36.4	1036	3108	2072	1347	1658	1243	1554
85	38.6	1085	3255	2170	1411	1736	1302	1628
90	40.9	1134	3402	2268	1474	1814	1361	1701
95	43.2	1183	3549	2366	1538	1893	1420	1775
100	45.5	1225	3675	2450	1593	1960	1470	1838
110	50	1260	3780	2520	1638	2016	1512	1890
120	54.5	1407	4221	2814	1829	2252	1688	2111
130	59.1	1491	4479	2982	1938	2386	1789	2237
140	63.6	1575	4725	3150	2048	2520	1890	2363
150	68.2	1659	4977	3318	2157	2654	1991	2489

APPENDIX D
RESOURCES

Brown, Steve. *Unlocking the Canine Ancestral Diet: Healthier Dog Food the ABCWway.* Dogwise Publishing, 2009.

Chandler, Marjorie L., and Gregg Takashima. "Nutritional Concepts for the Veterinary Practitioner." *Veterinary Clinics of North America: Small Animal Practice,* 44, no. 4 (2014): 645–666.

Davis, William. *Wheat Belly: Lose the Wheat, Lose the Weight, and Find Your Path Back to Health.* Rodale, 2011.

Dobson, Roy LM, Safa Motlagh, Mike Quijano, R. Thomas Cambron, Timothy R. Baker, Aletha M. Pullen, Brian T. Regg et al. "Identification and characterization of toxicity of contaminants in pet food leading to an outbreak of renal toxicity in cats and dogs." *Toxicological Sciences,* 106, no. 1 (2008): 251–262.

Dressler, Demian and Susan Ettinger. *The Dog Cancer Survival Fuide: Full-Spectrum Treatments to Optimize Your Dog's Life Quality and Longevity.* Maui Media, 2011.

Dzanis, David A. D.V.M., Ph.D., DACVN "Interpreting Pet Food Labels: Part 1: General Rules." FDA Veterinarian, November/December 1998 Vol. XIII No. VI. michigan.gov/documents/Interpreting_Pet_Food_Labels_-_Part_1_%28DD%29_125168_7.pdf

Dzanis, David A. D.V.M., Ph.D., DACVN "Interpreting Pet Food Labels: Part 2: Special Use Foods." FDA Veterinarian, January/February 1999, Vol. XIV, No. VI. michigan.gov/documents/Interpreting_Pet_Food_Labels_-_Part_2_%28DD%29_125169_7.pdf

Fascetti, Andrea J., and Sean J. Delaney, eds. *Applied Veterinary Clinical Nutrition.* John Wiley & Sons, 2012.

Harwell, Drew. "The McDonaldization of American pet food." *The Washington Post,* February 5, 2015.

Kealy et al. "Effects of diet restriction on life span and age-related changes in dogs." *Journal of the American Veterinary Medical Association,* 220, no. 9 (2002): 1315–1320.

Laflamme, Dorothy P., Gail Kuhlman, and Dennis F. Lawler. "Evaluation of weight loss protocols for dogs." *Journal of the American Animal Hospital Association,* 33, no. 3 (1996): 253–259.

Laflamme et al. "Myths and misperceptions about ingredients used in commercial pet foods." *Veterinary Clinics of North America: Small Animal Practice,* 44, no. 4 (2014): 689–698.

Lauten, Susan D. "Nutritional risks to large-breed dogs: from weaning to the geriatric years." *Veterinary Clinics of North America: Small Animal Practice,* 36, no. 6 (2006): 1345–1359.

Linder, Deborah, and Megan Mueller. "Pet obesity management: beyond nutrition." *Veterinary Clinics of North America: Small Animal Practice,* 44, no. 4 (2014): 789–806.

Lund et al. "Prevalence and risk factors for obesity in adult dogs from private US veterinary practices." *International Journal of Applied Research in Veterinary Medicine,* 4, no. 2 (2006): 177.

Mech, L. David, and Luigi Boitani, eds. *Wolves: Behavior, Ecology, and Conservation.* University of Chicago Press, 2010.

Nestle, Marion, and Malden Nesheim. *Feed Your Pet Right: The Authoritative Guide to Feeding Your Dog and Cat.* Simon and Schuster, 2010.

Pollan, Michael. *The Omnivore's Dilemma: A Natural History of Four Meals.* Penguin, 2006.

Raditic, D. M., R. L. Remillard, and K. C. Tater. "ELISA testing for common food antigens in four dry dog foods used in dietary elimination trials." *Journal of Animal Physiology and Animal Nutrition,* 95, no. 1 (2011): 90–97.

Segal AHCW, Monica, K9 Kitchen: Your Dog's Diet: The truth behind the Hype (2nd ed.) Self published, 2009.

Sizer et al. *Nutrition: Concepts and Controversies.* Cengage Learning, 2011.

Smith et al. "Lifelong diet restriction and radiographic evidence of osteoarthritis of the hip joint in dogs." *Journal of the American Veterinary Medical Association,* 229, no. 5 (2006): 690–693.

Tudor, Ken, DVM: hearthstonehomemade.com

Woolford, Rick. *Feed Your Best Friend Better: Easy, Nutritious Meals and Treats for Dogs.* Andrews McMeel Publishing April, 2012.

US AND EUROPEAN VETERINARY ASSOCIATIONS

American Animal Hospital Association
Nutritional assessment guidelines
www.aahanet.org/Library/NutritionalAsmt.aspx

American College of Veterinary Nutrition
Listing of board-certified veterinary nutritionists who will conduct nutritional consultations for veterinarians and/or pet owners
www.acvn.org

American College of Veterinary Nutrition
Listing of board-certified veterinary nutritionists who will formulate nutritionally balanced homemade diet recipes for veterinarians and/or pet owners
www.acvn.org

Association of American Feed Control (AAFCO)
Information on regulations, labeling, and other important facts
http://petfood.aafco.org

BalanceIT
Commercial website that offers semi-customized, balanced, home-cooked diet recipes for pet owners. Veterinarians can customize preformulated recipes for animals with medical conditions.
www.balanceit.com

Consumer's Guide to Pet Food
www.petfoodreport.com

Dietary Supplements Consumer Lab
Site (with a small subscription fee) that independently evaluates dietary supplements. Primarily for human supplements, but some pet supplements are included.
www.consumerlab.com

European College of Veterinary and Comparative Nutrition (ESVCN)
Veterinary nutritionists in Europe
www.esvcn.com

Federal Drug Administration (FDA)
Information, links, food safety issues, recalls, pet food labels
www.fda.gov/AnimalVeterinary/Products/AnimalFoodFeeds/PetFood/default.htm

National Research Council downloadable booklet
"Your Dog's Nutritional Needs"
http://dels-old.nas.edu/banr/petdoor.html

Pet Obesity Prevention
Useful information on assessing pets' body weight, calorie needs, and weight-loss tools
www.petobesityprevention.com

Pet Food Institute
Information on ingredient definitions, labeling regulations www.petfoodinstitute.org/Index.cfm?Page=Consumers

Pet Nutrition Alliance
Information and tools to increase awareness of the importance of optimal pet nutrition
www.petnutritionalliance.org

Tufts Cummings School of Veterinary Medicine
Raw diet fact sheet
www.tufts.edu/vet/nutrition/resources/raw_meat_diets.pdf

United States Department of Agriculture (USDA)
Food and nutrition information center: general supplement and nutrition information, links to a variety of dietary supplement websites
http://fnic.nal.usda.gov/nal_display/index.php?info_center=4&tax_level=1&tax_subject=274

World Small Animal Veterinary Association (WSMVA)
Nutritional assessment guidelines
www.wsava.org/educational/global-nutrition-committee

ABOUT THE AUTHOR

Greg Martinez, D.V.M., graduated from UC Davis in 1980. Fifteen years ago, he began to notice that adding healthy ingredients and avoiding irritating ones in commercial dog food and treats helped or even cured many chronic medical conditions such as itchy skin, ear infections, chronic diarrhea, and seizures. Since then, he has been passionate about educating his clients and pet owners about the many health benefits of feeding animals better ingredients.

He frequently posts to Facebook and Twitter as Dr. Greg DVM and has a channel on YouTube, Dr. Greg's Veterinary Views. He shares veterinary information on social media and nutritional information at dogdishdiet.com. Better-informed owners have healthier pets!

INDEX